Lutheranism, Anti-Judaism,
and Bach's *St. John Passion*

Lutheranism,

Anti-Judaism,

and Bach's

St. John Passion

WITH AN ANNOTATED LITERAL
TRANSLATION OF THE LIBRETTO

Michael Marissen

New York • Oxford

Oxford University Press

1998

Oxford University Press

Oxford   New York
Athens   Auckland   Bangkok   Bogota   Bombay
Buenos Aires   Calcutta   Cape Town   Dar es Salaam
Delhi   Florence   Hong Kong   Istanbul   Karachi
Kuala Lumpur   Madras   Madrid   Melbourne
Mexico City   Nairobi   Paris   Singapore
Taipei   Tokyo   Toronto   Warsaw

and associated companies in
Berlin   Ibadan

Copyright © 1998 by Oxford University Press, Inc.

Published by Oxford University Press, Inc.
198 Madison Avenue, New York, New York 10016

Oxford is a registered trademark of Oxford University Press

Library of Congress Cataloging-in-Publication Data
Marissen, Michael.
Lutheranism, anti-Judaism, and Bach's *St. John Passion* :
with an annotated literal translation of the libretto / Michael Marissen.
p.   cm.
Includes discography, bibliographical references, and indexes.
ISBN 0-19-511471-X
1. Bach, Johann Sebastian, 1685–1750. Johannespassion.
2. Bible. N.T. John XVIII–XIX.   German—Versions—Luther.
3. Jesus Christ—Passion—Role of Jews.   4. Lutheran Church—Relations—Judaism.
5. Judaism—Relations—Lutheran Church.   I. Bach, Johann Sebastian Bach, 1685–1750.
Johannespassion. Libretto. English & German.   II. Title.
ML410.B13M26   1998
782.23—dc21   97-40060

1 3 5 7 9 8 6 4 2

Printed in the United States of America
on acid-free paper

For Mary, Carl, and Zoë

Preface

This essay with annotated translation is designed for both general readers and scholars. I hope to have met the scholarly requirements of publications in history, musicology, and religion but have tried to write in such a way that the discussion will be readily comprehensible to readers with little or no background in any of these areas.

To accommodate those who do not read music, I have provided track numbers and timings of musical examples from various compact-disc recordings.

Full bibliographical titles are provided at the end in the list of Works Cited. Scriptural quotations are from the Calov Bible Commentary. Readers wishing to check citations need to know that versification and chapter divisions are similar but not identical in various Bibles.

In undertaking this study I would like to think that I have been motivated by what the motto of my graduate alma matter advocates, namely the search for "truth to its innermost parts." Readers are perhaps entitled, however, to know a little about my background experiences and what biases may stem from them. I grew up in Canada in a community of post-World War II Dutch Reformed immigrants, and studied music in the United States, first at Calvin College, an institution of the conservative Christian Reformed Church, and later at Brandeis University, a liberal secular Jewish institution. Bach was a focus of my work at both places, and I have come to take a particular interest in how his music reflects and shapes culture, especially in its religious aspects.

I understand that some people will be deeply suspicious of a Christian Bach scholar, no matter how open-minded or broadly ecumenical. The notion of the fully objective scholar, though, is a canard. And, moreover, any discussion involving the topic of Jesus' death surely cannot hope to be dispassionate. As Gerard Sloyan aptly puts it:

> In scholarly explorations of the crucifixion of Jesus — as considered separately from his resurrection by both religious believers and nonbelievers in it — it is impossible to discover dispassion, either intellectually conceived or as it touches the whole person. Too many claims have been made for this death, too many

lives have been lost both in witness to its meaning and as a tragically misguided conclusion from its meaning, for this dispassion to be possible.[1]

What I have striven for is thoroughness and honesty, all the while trying to watch out for what was expressed with such great wit in Laurence Sterne's _Tristram Shandy:_

> It is the nature of an hypothesis, when once a man has conceived it, that it assimilates everything to itself as proper nourishment; and, from the first moment of your begetting it, it generally grows the stronger by everything you see, hear, read, or understand. — This is of great use.[2]

I have not attempted to come up with what would result if a Lutheran, a Jew, an atheist, and an aesthete were imprisoned in the Music Division of the Library of Congress and given only bread and water until they reached a consensus on Bach.

I agree with those who contend that all scholarship is advocacy of some sort or another. Let me state up front what the principal concerns and assumptions of my "agenda" are: Music not only reflects but also forms culture. Great art lives on not because it is timeless but because it remains timely. Sometimes "purely" musical explanations may be inadequate for formally unconventional pieces — one should not just assume that matters of religion or religiosity in music are _extra_musical. Moreover, music has such wide appeal that discussion of challenging musical works may provide one of the best focal points for meaningful dialogue on the various sorts of issues raised by those works. (I am thinking primarily of dialogue among religious believers with nonbelievers, and among Jews with Christians.)

That last point has been decisive for me in structuring this study. Concert audiences of Bach's music, at least here in the United States, are remarkably diverse. And even among the self-designated members of various groups, I have found that there are astonishingly wide-ranging reactions to Bach's _St. John Passion._ Letting others know one's strong reactions to this work is very much on the rise, and some of the ensuing conversations have not been as productive as they could be, in part, it seems to me, because they stem from insensitivity and in part from weak knowledge of the work itself and its contexts.[3]

At first it seemed that the most appropriate way to structure the present discussion would be to follow the outline of a marvelous book title suggested by one of my colleagues: _John's Jews — Luther's John — Bach's Luther — Our Bach._ This would offer the considerable advantages of chronological

---

1. Sloyan, _Crucifixion of Jesus,_ 5.
2. Sterne, _Life and Opinions of Tristram Shandy,_ vol. 2, chap. 19, par. 26.
3. Public reception of the work after Bach's death has tended until recently either not to attend to religious issues at all or to engage only Lutheranism's more positive aspects.

movement and interpretive clarity. I decided against this progression, however, because I was concerned it might lend a false lucidity to the discussion.
Bach is, of course, the title's component that presumably most readers of
this study would want to call "ours." But for many readers there will also be
a significant sense of *our John,* not to mention *our Luther;* also, it seemed to
me that *Bach's John* was not necessarily identical to *Luther's John.* Risking
incoherence, I decided to discuss first *Bach's Luther-and-John,* then *Luther's
Jews,* then *Bach's Luther-and-Jews,* and finally *our Bach* with *"our" John;* references to *John's Jews* appear mostly only in footnotes in the libretto translation.

Some readers may wonder why this study bothers to cite historical biblical
criticism at all. If Bach essentially predates such interests, one might think
such research irrelevant to interpreting his music. Again, I believe Bach's
music is neither timeless nor trapped in its own epoch. Bach's music lives
on in part because it is able to speak to our contemporary needs and diverse
interests. The results of historical biblical research are only beginning to
reach the general public. I concluded that reporting on some aspects would
clarify interpretation of Bach's music, and I assumed it would be worth-
while to show that the results of responsible interpretation of Bach's music
are neither so far from nor so close to the historical Jesus as many readers
might expect.

Most of today's listeners pay no attention to the libretto of Bach's *St. John
Passion,* in large part because they uncritically assume that notes, tone colors, and rhythms are all that really matter. When people do turn attention
to the words, faulty knowledge can at times become a serious problem. For
example, some students with no knowledge of German have actually
opposed involvement with the *St. John Passion* on the grounds that it continually repeats the charge, "die, Jews!" (The text reads *die Jüden,* pronounced "dee YÜden," which actually means *"the* Jews.") More disturbingly, I have encountered remarkably strong resistance to the idea that
Bach's music even *might* be associated with antisemitism. Several musicians
have made remarks such as, "What is it with Jews anyway? The whole point
of great music is that it transcends anything you can put into words." I have
also heard Christian listeners say things like, "What they don't understand
is that Good Friday [the liturgical occasion for which the *St. John Passion*
was originally conceived] is our Holocaust."

I believe education and dialogue provide our best options for combating
ignorance and insensitivity. I very much hope the present study will do
more good than harm in promoting further discussion of the various issues
raised by Bach's music.

Acknowledgments

For providing financial support for this project, I am grateful to the National Endowment for the Humanities. For granting access to their various materials, I am also grateful to librarians at Swarthmore College, Princeton University, the Jewish Division of the New York Public Library, and the Lutheran Theological Seminary in Philadelphia. Thanks are due likewise to Don Franklin, Robin Leaver, and Joshua Rifkin for kindly making available out-of-the-way items from their personal libraries.

Of the great many people who have provided criticisms and encouragement (which is not to say that they necessarily endorse the views expressed here), I would like to thank especially John Alston, Jane Ambrose, John Butt, John Dominic Crossan, Gregory Crowell, Nathaniel Deutsch, Anthony Godzieba, Lydia Goehr, Bernard S. Greenberg, Susannah Heschel, Lawrence A. Hoffman, R. Po-Chia Hsia, Louis Kaplan, Howard Clark Kee, Leon Klenicki, Gavin I. Langmuir, Robin A. Leaver, Amy-Jill Levine, Robert L. Marshall, Daniel R. Melamed, Wilma Mosholder, George W. Nickelsburg, Heiko A. Oberman, Adele Reinhartz, Joshua Rifkin, Lawrence A. Rosenwald, Franklin Sherman, Calvin Stapert, Renate Steiger, Frances Stier, Richard Taruskin, Linwood Urban, Alexandra Volin, Mark I. Wallace, and Timothy J. Wengert.

I have also learned a great deal from delivering parts of the study as lectures at various institutions. For their invitations I would like to thank Ruth van Baak Griffioen (Music Department, College of William and Mary), Scott Balthazar (Mid-Atlantic Chapter of the American Musicological Society), Karol Berger (Music Department, Stanford University), John Butt with Richard Taruskin (Music Department, University of California at Berkeley), Robert Gross with Sharon Friedler (Deans' Office with Department of Music and Dance at Swarthmore College), Paul Horsley with Murray Friedman (Philadelphia Orchestra with American Jewish Committee), E. Ann Matter (Department of Religious Studies, University of Pennsylvania), Sterling Murray (Music History Department, West Chester University), Kenneth Slowik (Oberlin College Conservatory of Music — Baroque Performance Institute), Jeannette Sorrell with Susannah Heschel (*Apollo's Fire* with Samuel Rosenthal Center for Judaic Studies at Case Western Reserve University), and Anne Stone with George Nickelsburg (School of Music with School of Religion, University of Iowa).

Without the friendship and support of my spouse, Mary, this study would never have been completed, and it is dedicated to her and our children, Carl and Zoë.

Swarthmore, Pennsylvania   M. M.
Spring 1997

Contents

Lutheranism, Anti-Judaism,
and Bach's *St. John Passion*

Lutheranism, Anti-Judaism, and Bach's *St. John Passion*

> I have my brothers among the Turks, Papists, Jews, and all peoples. Not that they are
> Turks, Jews, Papists, and Sectaries or will remain so; in the evening they will be called
> into the vineyard and given the same wage as we. (Sebastian Franck, 16th century)

Although the bibliographies on Bach and on Judaica have grown enor-
mously since World War II, there has been very little work on relationships
between these two areas. It is not difficult to account for this. History, religion, and sociology scholars who focus on issues of antisemitism often lack
musical training and are, in any event, quite reasonably interested in even
more pressing social and political manifestations. Bach scholars, on the
other hand, have largely pursued more narrowly musical topics such as nota-
tion, form, style, attribution, and chronology. A small branch has concerned
itself with Bach and Lutheran theology, but its practitioners have generally
centered on the librettos without paying much attention to the ways that
the words are set musically. Strangely, almost no scholarly attention has
been given to relationships between Lutheranism and the religion of
Judaism as they affect Bach's most problematic work in this respect, the *St.
John Passion*. The only studies are in German, and, although each makes
far-reaching observations about Luther, none of them adequately engages
Bach's music.[1]

Luther's scathingly polemic writings are fairly well known today.[2] Because
Bach's indebtedness to Luther has come to be more widely acknowledged,
listeners can easily assume that Bach harbored hostility to Jews and,
accordingly, that his music probably projects such hostility. Many other
listeners, however, believe Bach produced great music which transcends any
sort of verbally specifiable meaning. Interpretive Bach research might
reasonably be expected to have engaged these difficult issues more fully by
now. Through a reappraisal of Bach's work and its contexts, I do not so
much aim to provide definitive answers as to present information and

---

1. Hoffmann-Axthelm, "Bach und die *perfidia Iudaica*"; Steiger, "Wir haben keinen
König"; Walter, "Die Bibel, Bach, die Juden."
2. Especially his "On the Jews and their Lies" of 1543. One should not assume that
Lutheranism at any given time and place would necessarily replicate Luther's views on a given
subject; see, e.g., Wallmann, "Reception of Luther's Writings on the Jews." Luther had written more positive things about Jews in his earlier writings (e.g., in "That Jesus Christ was
born a Jew" of 1523). But even though Luther expressed extreme contempt only in his later
writings, he never saw Judaism as a legitimate system of beliefs and practices. He had imagined that more Jews would embrace a reformed Christianity than did. See also the discussion
here at pp. 23–27.

3

interpretive commentary that could serve as a basis for more informed and sensitive discussion.

The discussion here will center first on what I gather are the principal messages of Bach's *St. John Passion:* Jesus' identity and work, and the effect of these on the lives of his followers. Further discussion of these principal messages will bring us to the issue of the gospel of John and hostility to Jews. I will suggest that fostering hostility to Jews is not the subject or purpose of Bach's interpretation of the gospel's passion narrative. In so structuring the discussion, I do not mean to suggest that whatever one makes of questions raised in the first half of the essay must necessarily affect what one concludes about those addressed only in the second.

Issues of Method

What are the messages of Bach's *St. John Passion?* We will consider some background information on how the work came into being, on what the piece seems to be saying, and how it could have been understood by its original listeners. The approach adopted here will not by any means exhaust the work's meanings. I have operated on the assumption that responsible modern interpretation will give serious attention to historical contexts, and that this ought to affect whatever else we might bring to the work. In other words, I am viewing this in terms of classical hermeneutics, familiar from several centuries of biblical interpretation. The task is to figure out not only what Bach's music probably meant to its first audiences, but also how we can attempt to reconcile their historical and our modern concerns. In this view, each must affect the other to interpret with ethical intelligence.

Some people are exclusively interested in the first pole — what original meanings are likely to have been — and thus, it could be argued, are essentially antiquarians. On the other hand, many people swing to the other side of the continuum and perhaps over-emphasize the second pole: present interests. It seems to me that if we focus exclusively or too prominently on our own concerns and conceptions, we end up simply appropriating the past and do not allow ourselves truly to learn anything.

One way this latter problem often surfaces is for listeners to relegate any religious qualities to the past and to attend only to the aesthetic qualities of Bach's notes, rhythms, and tone colors. (I would say that Bach's music speaks powerfully to both aims; his works stand neither solely as religious nor solely as nonverbal aesthetic documents.) It is commonplace today to think of Bach's music as great art which is best listened to "for its own sake," and that this must have been the composer's intention too. But this modern, cherished notion of art is certainly unhistorical for Bach.[3] In his teachings on keyboard playing, for example, Bach remarked, "[The basso continuo makes] a well-sounding harmony to the honor of God and to the sanctioned enjoyment of the spirit;[4] the aim and final reason, as of all music, so of the basso continuo, should be none else but the honor of God and the refreshing of the mind."[5] Thinking that art should merely be beautiful or magnificent may help us to feel pleased by Bach's music, but it does not necessarily help much in understanding it. That is to say, there is no longer any point in questioning or discussing Bach's artistic greatness, something both widely accepted and exceedingly difficult to explain. Issues of meaning, however, cannot be dismissed by appealing to aesthetics.

Preferring the idea that the so-called extramusical aspects of the *St. John Passion* ought to be ignored is perhaps like the main character's pleasurable experiences of Italian and Russian in the movie *A Fish Called Wanda:* she is invariably stimulated by their sounds but shows no interest in learning the languages. My intent here, however, is not categorically to condemn listeners who wish to contemplate the *St. John Passion's* great beauty or magnificence, but rather to ask why it is that such works are said in common parlance to have "pure beauty" (that is to say, verbally specifiable meanings, such as those involving religious or other agendas, are deemed foreign to the point of the work, and all textual or contextual matters are uncritically labelled "*extra*musical"). How is it, for example, that one can maintain a straight face while protesting the irruption of religion or religiosity into Bach's music when it was designed for religious purposes and, furthermore, when many of its religious sentiments, and whatever religious and social benefits or problems might attend them, have by no means passed into "history"? It is one thing to say that *Bach and religious sentiment* is a story we are not interested in, but another to say that *Bach and pure aesthetic contemplation* is a better and more authentic story.[6]

3. For an excellent general introduction to Bach's views of music, see Taruskin, "Facing Up," 309–14.

4. Bach's words here are *zulässiger Ergötzung des Gemüths*. In modern German, *ergötzen* has largely taken on the meaning "to amuse," or "to entertain," but in eighteenth-century usage it meant "to bring about palpable joy." See Adelung, *Grammatisch-kritisches Wörterbuch*, 1894, who provides several examples for its usage, mostly from the Bible, none of which has to do with entertainment or diversion. The word is used in this more edifying sense each time it appears in Bach's church cantatas.

5. Spitta, *Johann Sebastian Bach*, vol. 2, 916. These teachings are based on the writings of Friedrich Erhard Niedt. Some entries in the manuscript of Bach's version have recently been identified as the handwriting of one of Bach's students in Leipzig; see Schulze, *Studien zur Bach-Überlieferung*, 125–27.

6. See, e.g., Schulenberg, "'Musical Allegory' Reconsidered," 238: "As modern listeners attending to old music, we perform a sort of deconstruction of the work's official purpose, rediscovering [*sic*] that another purpose, perhaps even the most important purpose, of the

Some Performance Considerations

With the *St. John Passion*'s range of hermeneutically plausible meanings being far from straightforward for the majority of today's listeners, it could be considered irresponsible to render the work without an accurate translation and informed program notes or spoken commentary and discussion of some sort. I am referring here primarily to recordings or concert performances at educational or cultural institutions. In these situations, listeners may or may not think about the work's messages or find themselves affected by them. There is no assumption that the performers or the audiences endorse the messages. But in any event, I would say that the messages should not be overlooked, and that performances ought to include critical commentary of some sort. Whether it is fair to assume that students are intellectually and emotionally prepared to perform in concert, as opposed to study only via recordings, challenging works of this sort should also be considered carefully.

A fully liturgical rendering of the work in church raises somewhat different issues. In a service, although some people might attend to listen to the music for its own sake, the expectation is that the congregation does accept all or most of the liturgy's messages. Here, fuller contextual commentary on the passion narrative will almost certainly happen as a matter of course (in the pastor's sermon). Although performances of the *St. John Passion* in concert and on recordings are fairly common, fully liturgical renderings in church services are exceedingly rare. Most churches nowadays, even assuming they could meet the considerable expenses, would not welcome the idea of extending a service to include a two-hour piece of music.

If the *St. John Passion* for some reason has to be performed without providing an educational context, I suggest that any passages easily running the risk of giving serious offence might be carefully excised or altered but acknowledged as such in the program in order to avoid accusations of censorship.[7] On the other hand, I can also understand those who, whether or not they consider the original words offensive, might find any so-motivated altering of artworks intellectually and emotionally insulting. The best

---

music may not be didactic or devotional but aesthetic: it aims to please, not to instruct or inspire, even if the latter is what Baroque ideology directed. . . . In modern terms, the works [of composers like Bach] are amoral and meaningless: above all, politically incorrect." Does it even make sense to say something can be politically incorrect *and* amoral and meaningless?

7. I agree with Richard Taruskin's recommendations on how to perform antisemitic music responsibly ("Text and Act," 357–58) but disagree with his passing observation that places Bach's *St. John Passion* on the list of artworks possibly embodying an inhumanity designed to reinforce antisemitism ("Text and Act," 358); see also Marty, "Art that Offends."

approach, I believe (from conviction and personal experience), is not to alter the work but to provide critical commentary.

Some listeners may find the sheer sound of the work repugnant: the phonemes of the German language seem menacing, no matter what words they form — the German language carries the sins of the Third Reich for many people still alive. Here there will be few easy solutions (e.g., performing the work in translation introduces a host of new difficulties). Nonetheless, educational commentary and discussion, even if unresolved, is the best way to go.

I do not claim, either, to have any sense of what is the right thing to do for listeners for whom no amount of contextual understanding of Bach's particular interpretation of John will prevent the gospel from being construed against the Jewish people any less forcefully now than ever. Granting that historians, theologians, and musicologists often have a startlingly naive optimism about the ability of scholarship to mediate in conflicts of opinion or belief, I have come to the conclusion that it would be better to engage the issues critically than to say nothing or to make vain pleas for an end to the performance of Bach's music and the proclamation of John's gospel.

In brief: to musical aesthetes — who would reduce Bach's powerful work to the artistry of its notes, rhythms, and tone colors — and also to listeners who find Bach's music deeply meaningful but may not have considered its attendant religious and cultural issues, I hope to show that interpreting the *St. John Passion* might be more problematic than they think. To those who assume the work essentially teaches hostility to Jews, I hope likewise to show that interpreting this work might be more problematic than they think.

Bach's Duties

It was Bach's job as Cantor at the St. Thomas School of Leipzig to be a musical preacher for the city's main churches. Before taking up his duties in 1723 he was successfully tested on his knowledge of and commitment to Lutheran theology and the Bible by Johann Schmid (professor of theology at the University of Leipzig) and, separately, by Salomon Deyling (professor of theology at the University of Leipzig, superintendent of the Leipzig churches, and pastor at the St. Nicholas Church).[8] In this connection, it is worth noting that a list of titles from Bach's large personal library of Bible commentaries and sermons survives;[9] and his own copy of the Calov Bible

8. Neumann, *Bach-Dokumente II*, 99–101; some of this is translated in David, *Bach Reader*, 92–93.
9. Leaver, *Bachs Theologische Bibliothek*, 36–41.

Commentary, with Bach's many hand-penned entries, is now kept at the Concordia Seminary Library in St. Louis, Missouri.[10]

Although it is not known for certain who compiled the poetry for the *St. John Passion*,[11] it was in any event Bach's responsibility to submit copies of his proposed librettos to the superintendent of the Leipzig churches well in advance so that their theological and seasonal appropriateness could be confirmed and so that they could then be printed for distribution to churchgoers.[12] The *St. John Passion* libretto consists of Luther's translation of John's biblical narrative verbatim in the forms of recitatives and choruses, along with other writers' extensive poetic commentaries on it in the forms of chorales and arias. Bach's setting serves to amplify and deepen the verbal messages of the libretto and, at times, to suggest different meanings for the words than they might have if they were simply read. The words and the notes, then, together form a sort of polyphony, and it is this that I would prefer to call the "music." Bach's duties, to which he agreed in writing before assuming his post at Leipzig, were to compose music that "should thus be created so as not to appear *opera*-centered [e.g., reveling in vocal technique simply for its own sake, presenting music more for effect than edification], but, much more, to incite the listeners to devotion."[13]

The *St. John Passion* was not designed as a self-contained concert work but as part of a liturgical church service with other music, prayers, an extended sermon, and so on.[14] Some information about the contemporary Leipzig prayers and hymns is available,[15] but unfortunately the pastoral sermons preached along with them at Bach's churches are not.

For fuller explanation of the music's theological concerns, I will be drawing continually upon the two main Lutheran biblical commentaries in Bach's personal library, the massive volumes of Calov and Olearius.[16] This

---

10. Facsimiles of the pages with Bach's notations are found in Cox, *Calov Bible,* 108–393.

11. Several versions of Bach's *St. John Passion* survive. The libretto printed and discussed here is the one from the version put on the most often. The other versions are almost never rendered. Convenient guides through the bewilderingly complex information on the various versions can be found in Schulze, *Bach Compendium,* 985–93; and Dürr, *Johannes-Passion,* 13–26.

12. Petzoldt, *Texte zur Leipziger Kirchen-Musik,* 12–19.

13. Neumann, *Bach-Dokumente I,* 177: "die *Music . . .* auch also beschaffen seyn möge, damit sie nicht *opern*hafftig herauskommen, sondern die Zuhörer viehlmehr zur Andacht aufmuntere." Secular material could be and was co-opted for liturgical use (witness Bach's continual resetting of his own secular cantatas with new liturgical texts); the point is that church music, however similar it might be to secular music, should be spiritually uplifting and not merely entertaining.

14. Leaver, *J. S. Bach,* 8–26.

15. Terry, *Joh. Seb. Bach: Cantata Texts,* 208–9.

16. Calov, *Die heilige Bibel;* Olearius, *Biblische Erklärung.* I claim in citing these writers not proof for my arguments but contextual plausibility. In discussing Bach's study of the

procedure should not be taken, however, to undercut the profundities of John's gospel itself or Bach's music. To readers who might be concerned that the present discussion will be overly theological, I should spell out that I am presenting merely what I gather is the projected theology of the *St. John Passion.* That is to say, I will not be weighing religious truth claims.

Lutheranism and Theories of Atonement

The gospel of John and Bach's *St. John Passion* give expression to several Christian views of God's reconciliation with humanity. There has been a great deal of discussion in the history of Christian thought over which of these ideas of atonement works best, how the ideas are related to each other, who came up with them, who made which modifications to them, and so on. There is also currently no complete agreement on which views Luther and early Lutheranism most desired to promote. For our purposes, however, it will suffice simply to indicate briefly some features of these three standard ideas and how they appear to correspond to the sentiments expressed in the *St. John Passion.*

One of these views, often referred to as the *Christus Victor* or "classic" theory,[17] involves perhaps the greatest paradox in all theology and history: divine glory defined as deepest abasement; "the Word became flesh" to die on the cross. This paradox was important to Luther's development of the "theology of the cross," the notion that to humans God reveals himself only "hidden" in the lowliness of the crucifixion. In this theory of atonement, victory has been secured by Jesus in the cosmic battle between God and the demonic powers of evil. Followers of Jesus participate in the truth of this victory. As we shall see later (pp. 18–20), the *St. John Passion* gives especially powerful expression to the classic theory in its commentary on John 19:30a, the aria no. 30, *"Es ist vollbracht."*

Calov Bible, I do not mean to suggest that there was some sort of causal connection between his highlighting the various Lutheran commentaries and his composing the *St. John Passion* in 1724. For one thing, even if Bach indeed owned this Bible before 1733 (Herz, "J. S. Bach 1733," 255–63), he probably obtained it only after 1725 (Dürr, *Johannes-Passion,* 52); and for another thing, we do not know in many cases when Bach's underlinings and marginalia were entered. There are many apparent connections with Olearius in the *St. John Passion,* and, so far as I can tell, there is no reason to doubt that Bach owned or had access to this commentary before 1724 (see also the annotation for this entry in the list of Works Cited). On the importance of Olearius for the compilation of the *St. John Passion* libretto, see Franklin, "Libretto of Bach's John Passion."

17. See Aulén, *Christus Victor,* 17–96, 117–38. See also Pelikan, *Bach Among the Theologians,* 74–88, 102–15. For a fuller introduction to the standard Christian theories of atonement, see Urban, *A Short History of Christian Thought,* 101–24.

Another view, often referred to as the "Latin" or "satisfaction" theory, takes Jesus' crucifixion to be the "perfect sacrifice." This sacrifice is called perfect because it was the voluntary offering of a sinless person. (Because he is divine, the man Jesus was sinless, and because, being sinless, he did not otherwise have to die, his sacrifice was voluntary.) Reparation for the sins of humankind has been made, and God the Father's mercy and wrath do not have to operate unrestrained. Images of sacrifice appear throughout the gospel of John, and some particulars of John's passion narrative differ from the other canonical gospels,[18] probably in part to promote the idea of Jesus as the "Passover lamb."[19] In Lutheranism, John 19:29 ("hyssop[20]") and 19:36 ("break no bone[21]") were taken as paschal lamb imagery, harking back to John 1:29 and 1:36. Luther understood something of the Hidden God to be at work here as well: although the crucified Jesus looks like a base criminal, he is in fact the divine (sinless) sacrificial "Lamb of God."[22] The *St. John Passion* employs explicit sacrificial language in its commentary on John 19:30b, the aria with chorale, *"Mein teurer Heiland,"* no. 32 ("you, who made propitiation for me . . . Give me only what you have merited").

A third view, often called the "ethical" theory, takes the incarnation itself (God's entering human life in the person of Jesus) to express God's love for humanity. In this theory, Jesus' crucifixion frees humans from slavery to sin and thereby gives them the freedom to love each other. One of the central biblical texts is John 15:12–13, where Jesus is depicted as saying, "This is my commandment, that you love one another as I have loved you. No one has greater love than this, to lay down his life for his friends." The *St. John Passion* employs this theory's language in nos. 3, 17, and perhaps 39 but

18. Luther, *Das 18. und 19. Kapitel,* 202–3: "But after Jesus had finished his prayer [John 17], he becomes the priest, and offers the proper offering, namely himself on the wood of the cross: this is the Passion [narrative], which St. John describes somewhat differently from the other gospel writers."

19. Technically, this incorporates the sacrificial lamb of Passover (which breaks the power of death; Exodus 12) and the sacrificial goat of the Day of Atonement (which takes away the sins of the people; Leviticus 16); cf. I Corinthians 5:7 and 15:3. This is not to say that the Exodus and Leviticus passages do fully support the satisfaction theory. See Sloyan, *Crucifixion of Jesus,* 61–62, 99–102.

20. See n. 71 in the Annotated Literal Translation.

21. See n. 81 in the Annotated Literal Translation.

22. Luther, *Das 18. und 19. Kapitel,* 388: "But what this passage [John 19:17], [stating] that Christ was killed outside the city at the Place of Skulls, has hidden [or, "has for a mystery" — *für ein Geheimnis hat*] is shown by the Epistle to the Hebrews at chap. 13 [vs. 11], with these words: 'animals whose blood is brought into the sanctuary by the high priest as a sacrifice for sin are to be burned outside the camp' [vs. 12: 'Therefore Jesus also suffered outside the city gate in order to sanctify the people by his own blood']." At p. 406, commenting on John 19:30, Luther combines language of victory and sacrifice (quoted in Calov, *Die heilige Bibel,* V, 947).

most prominently in its commentary on John 19:27a, the chorale stanza, *"Er nahm alles wohl in acht,"* no. 28 ("O humankind, set everything in order, love God and humankind, die afterwards without any woe").

Following Jesus, According to the *St. John Passion*

Let us turn now to closer consideration of how the music of Bach's *St. John Passion* projects religious sentiments.

Who Is Jesus?

The gospel of John continually refers to Jesus as the "Son of God" and "King of Israel," and it places great stock in Jesus' divine nature. Unlike other biblical accounts, which place a somewhat greater emphasis on his human nature, the gospel of John portrays Jesus as having no doubts; he always seems to know what is going to happen to him and welcome it. People are led to recognize who Jesus is (in Lutheran language, to see his divinity with and behind his humanity), and they are freed from sin by his priestly sacrifice and glorious victory over death in the crucifixion.

The opening chorus of Bach's *St. John Passion* powerfully lays out the Johannine beliefs that glorification is inextricably linked with abasement and that Jesus participates in the Godhead. The first two lines are based on Psalm 8 from the Hebrew Scriptures,[23] which read "how glorious is your name [*Name,* not *Ruhm*] in all the lands." Olearius writes concerning Psalm 8: "glorious is your name and praise" (*herrlich ist dein Nahme und Ruhm*).[24] Bach's music projects a strong sense of *verherrlichen* and *rühmen* as two theologically related types of glorifying, the latter referring to glory in the sense of "to make known," and the former in the sense of "to make Godlike," i.e.,

---

23. I will employ the standard term "Hebrew Scriptures" to refer to what in the confessional language of Christianity is usually called the Old Testament. Protestantism's first testament contains the same books as the Hebrew Bible ("Tanakh"), but the ordering, numbering, and the chapter and verse divisions are not identical. (Greek, Roman Catholic, and Slavonic Bibles include additional books in their Old Testaments.) There is as yet no generally accepted and understood non-supersessionist term for Christianity's apostolic writings, the New Testament.

24. Olearius, *Biblische Erklärung,* III, 56; cf. Bach's setting of Psalm 48:10 ("God, as your name, so is also your praise [reaching] to the ends of the earth") in the church cantata *Gott, wie dein Name, so ist auch dein Ruhm* (BWV 171).

"to suffer" (*ver*herr*lichen*).[25] The form this interest takes in the *St. John Passion* perhaps owes something to Olearius. In his commentaries on John, Olearius several times calls attention to Jesus' glorification through "deepest abasement [*tiefster Erniedrigung*]," often referring to Psalm 8.[26] The Calov Commentary Bible reads at the heading for Psalm 8: "Herr Luther . . . sums up [this psalm] in the following way: it is a prophecy of Christ, his suffering [on the cross], resurrection, and ruling over all creatures, . . . a kingdom established not by sword and armor but by word and faith."[27]

In Bach's setting, which likewise takes a christocentric reading of the psalm, the choir exclaims the libretto's single *Herr* often in groups of three, possibly evoking Jesus within the Trinity: *"Herr* [Father], *Herr* [Son], *Herr* [Holy Spirit]." The texture of the orchestral introduction might also be considered trinitarian: long, tortured, dissonant notes by the woodwinds (Son);[28] short, whirling notes by the strings that eventually migrate to other voices (Holy Spirit); and medium-length, repeated notes by the bass instruments (Father) (Ex. 1: Kuijken,[29] CD 1, track 1, 0:00–1:27). Martin Geck notes that during Bach's lifetime a side altar of the St. Nicholas Church in Leipzig, where the *St. John Passion* was first rendered, displayed Lucas Cranach the Elder's 1515 painting The Holy Trinity; Jesus, his body still cruciform, rests glorified in the arms of the Father, who is seated on the Throne of Grace, while the Holy Spirit in the form of a dove lands on Jesus' knee.[30] Bach's opening chorus appears likewise to focus on Jesus' identity, projecting that not only is he Christ, but he is also God ("Lord, our *ruler* . . . show us . . . that you, the *true Son of God,* have . . . been glorified"). In fact, the *St. John Passion* is probably unique among contemporary passion settings in having its opening chorus focus not so much on what the passion means for the redemption of humanity but rather on the nature of Jesus.[31] In theological language, christology is emphasized over soteriology, but only here at the outset of the work.

25. See Marissen, "Theological Character of Bach's *Musical Offering,*" 87, 101–5. For more concerning the theological character of even Bach's secular instrumental music, see also Marissen, *Social and Religious Designs,* 111–19, passim.

26. Olearius, *Biblische Erklärung,* V, 775–76, 782, 788, 792.

27. Calov, *Die heilige Bibel,* II, 256–57.

28. Cf. the comments on no. 21d at n. 42 in the Annotated Literal Translation.

29. In the main text all musical examples will be drawn from this good, widely available, and inexpensive recording. In Appendix 2 all of the examples are also listed by their measure numbers and with their tracks and timings from other selected recordings. Any college library or good CD shop should have available at least one of these recordings.

30. Both Bach's trinitarian texture and Cranach's painting are noted and contextualized in Geck, *Johannespassion,* 46–49.

31. Axmacher, *"Aus Liebe will mein Heiland Sterben,"* 164.

In the biblical narrative that follows, there are various subtle ways that the issue of Jesus' identity and power are represented by Bach's music. To explore this I will be noting internal and external associations for various pieces from Bach's setting. Readers should not assume that these associations inevitably call for the interpretive deductions I draw from them. There is a massive bibliography of previous writings on the *St. John Passion.*[32] I hope that whatever new ideas are presented here will be judged by the criterion of relative explanatory power, not of irrevocability. (Very few interpretations can truly be shown to be necessary rather than more or less plausible.)

When his assailants arrive on the scene, Jesus does not wait but goes out to meet them, a detail not found in the other canonical gospels. Jesus asks, "Whom do you seek"; they answer, "Jesus of Nazareth"; he replies, *Ich bin's.* Jesus does not mean simply "it's me."[33] Jesus speaks as God. He echoes God's "absolute usage" of "I AM" (in John's Greek, *ego eimi*), familiar from the story in Exodus 3 of God's appearing to Moses from a burning bush.[34] Because Jesus' *Ich bin's* is a divine utterance (a theophany), all those in his presence fall involuntarily to the ground. Olearius discusses *Ich bin's* extensively, noting:

> I am the one. The Son of the Living God . . . *n.b.* Exodus 3:14. . . . "I am the one, who I am" [*Ich bins, der Ich bin*]. . . . At this omnipotent, powerful Word [*Ich bins*], suddenly, as by thunder, they would be struck down, so that they fell to the ground. It was a view of Godly majesty and glory [*Herrlichkeit*] — John 1:14, therefore here [John 18] vs. 8.[35]

Bach sets Jesus' I AM (at no. 2c) so that both the melody and the supporting harmony move from the fifth to the first positions in a scale with G as its home pitch, something hereafter to be called "V–I cadence in G" (Ex. 2: Kuijken, CD 1, track 4, 0:00–0:07). The cadence's forcefulness and simplicity give Jesus' answer as firm, unequivocal, and non-evasive a tone as is possible in the musical language of the eighteenth century. Later, for interpretive purposes, Bach's music will refer to the I AM by employing an identical or nearly identical cadence. (This striking formula can easily be recalled

32. Wolff, *Bach-Bibliographie;* Nestle, "Bachschrifttum 1981 bis 1985"; Nestle, "Bachschrifttum 1986 bis 1990." An on-line bibliography of writings on Bach has been established by Yo Tomita but was not yet available as of this writing (it can be found at *http://www.music.qub.ac.uk/~tomita/bachbib.html*).

33. In German-speaking countries today the conventional reply to someone's *Wer ist's?* ("who is it?") following your knocking on their door is *Ich bin's* ("it's me").

34. For a convenient and concise introduction to biblical *ego eimi* usage, see Brown, *Introduction to New Testament Christology,* 137–41.

35. Olearius, *Biblische Erklärung,* V, 776.

by listeners.)[36] Through these means, Bach's music will be able to express how this issue, the identity of Jesus of Nazareth, is one upon which other key theological questions hinge: discipleship and freedom of the Christian as found by grace through faith, not good works (a New Testament concept of Paul's, as interpreted by Luther).

During Jesus' trial, Pilate, the Roman prefect of Judaea, asks Jesus (at no. 18a), "So you are a king, then?" This question follows upon a great deal of Jesus' elusive talk about his kingdom's being not of this world and so forth. Pilate is having a difficult time figuring out whether Jesus represents some sort of troublemaker or is simply a harmless lunatic. Jesus answers, *Du sagst's, ich bin ein König* ("You say that I am a king"). He sings *Du sagst's* ("*you* say it") unmistakably like the I AM cadence centered on G heard at the beginning of the passion narrative, at John 18:5.[37] Bach's musical text — even more strikingly Johannine than John's actual verbal text — thus has Jesus saying "I AM *the* king himself"[38] (Ex. 3: Kuijken, CD 1, track 27, 0:00–0:21). The question is whether this Truth will be recognized, thus making doubly ironic Pilate's question, at no. 18a, "What is truth?" The issues reflected by Jesus' I AM language greatly concern Pilate's Jewish subjects, for they surely were not led to expect a messiah for whom there would also be claims of divinity from him or his followers.[39]

The music's *ego eimi* motivic formula brings out something that is not so clearly expressed in the libretto itself, namely the issue of which character is really in charge of the proceedings in the narrative. This takes a bit of explanation. The very first time we hear from Pilate (near the beginning of Part Two), he sings a melodic formula that will return whenever he makes statements concerning law. At the syllables *Kla-ge wi-der die-sen Men-schen* in no. 16a, he climbs to a D, falls from D to B to G-sharp, and closes by rising stepwise to C, over a V–I cadence with A as the home pitch (Ex. 4: Kuijken, CD 1, track 21, 0:21–0:34). He sings the same formula at the syllables *rich-tet ihn nach eu-rem Ge-set-ze* in no. 16c (Ex. 5: Kuijken, CD 1, track 23, 0:00–0:09) and at *daß ich euch ei-nen los-ge-be* in no. 18a (Ex. 6: Kuijken, CD 1, track 27, 1:02–1:18), each time again with A as the home pitch, in the former instance with a rapid shift in tonal center to effect the move to A. The very first thing Pilate says to Jesus during the trial (in no. 16e) is, *Bist du der Jüdenkönig?* ("Are you the King of the Jews?"), and Jesus

---

36. Although it is entirely conventional in Bach's recitative style to mark off sentences with V–I harmonies, it is unusual — especially repeatedly through a work — for the melody itself to move from the fifth to first degrees of the scale rather than the second or seventh to first.

37. Olearius (*Biblische Erklärung*, V, 781) links these two passages as well.

38. See also the comments on Jesus' words "Behold, these same ones know what I have said" at n. 18 in the Annotated Literal Translation.

39. Cf. n. 54 in the Annotated Literal Translation.

replies, *Redest du das von dir selbst, oder haben's dir andere von mir gesagt?* ("Do you speak of that on your own initiative, or have others said it to you about me?"). Since Pilate's music had just shifted to the key of G at this point, there was a perfect setup for Jesus to answer, "I am," over a V–I cadence in G. Jesus does sing *Redest du* on the fifth and first pitches in G but immediately works it into the melody of *Soll ich den Kelch nicht trinken* (no. 4, "shall I not drink the cup") before quickly shifting to A as the home pitch. This enables him to sing the syllables *o-der ha-ben's dir an-de-re von mir ge-sagt?* to the recurring melodic formula of Pilate's law statements (Ex. 7: Kuijken, CD 1, track 25, 0:31–0:48). Bach's music for *oder haben's dir andere von mir gesagt* ("or have others said it to you about me?"), it seems to me, thereby conveys the message, more demonstrably than the libretto does by itself, that Jesus is not merely answering Pilate's question with another (annoying) question — rather, by appropriating an idiosyncratic melody otherwise associated only with Pilate's law statements, Jesus is also putting Pilate on trial. Will he follow "the Truth," namely Jesus himself?[40] Are listeners supposed to recall John 3:19–21, where Jesus speaks of people being judged by their reaction to him, "the light of the world"?

Faith and Discipleship

There is another series of melodic allusions that comes out of this kingship idea and that touches upon issues of discipleship.

Just before Pilate turns Jesus over to be crucified, the Roman soldiers dress him in a purple (i.e., regal) robe, crown him with thorns, and call out, derisively, "Greetings, dear King of the Jews!"[41] (no. 21b; Ex. 8: Kuijken, CD 2, track 2, 0:00–0:34). This chorus is in the same key and has the same melodic shape as the beginning of the soprano aria "I will follow you likewise" (no. 9; Ex. 9: Kuijken, CD 1, track 12, 0:21–0:39). The aria's theme in turn has the same contour as Bach's setting of the words *Simon Petrus aber folgete Jesu nach* ("Simon Peter, however, followed Jesus") in the

40. See also the comments on Jesus' words "You would have no power over me, if it were not handed down to you from on high" at n. 47 in the Annotated Literal Translation.

41. Luther and some modern commentators explicitly note that the *stratiotes* (soldiers) of John 19 were Roman (see n. 6 in the Annotated Literal Translation). That the soldiers were not Jews is evident from the fact that the soldiers later (nos. 21a–21c) mock Jesus inside the hall of judgment. ("The Jews," according to no. 16a, do "not go in the hall of judgment, lest they would be defiled, but that they might eat the Passover meal.") The soldiers' "Greetings, dear King of the Jews!" has always been understood as mockery. It should perhaps be noted that when Crossan says there is in John's passion narrative no mockery of Jesus before or during his death (*Who Killed Jesus?*, 141, 146), Crossan is not referring to this passage but only to when Jesus is on the cross.

previous recitative (no. 8; Ex. 10: Kuijken, CD 1, track 11, 0:00–0:11). With B-flat as the home pitch, nos. 8, 9, and 21b move melodically up from F to B-flat, continue up stepwise to F, down to B-flat or D, and up to G. The aria and chorus (nos. 9 and 21b) then go on to move downwards by step from G to B-flat and close on D to C.

The melodic shape of the soprano aria captures an irony extremely well: the recitative said "Peter . . . followed Jesus," and the aria declares "I will 'follow' [Jesus] likewise." I (i.e., the "existential I," the listener to the narrative), like Peter, cheerfully declare to Jesus that I am his follower; but actually, just as Peter is about to do, I will continually deny my discipleship and *not* follow Jesus.

Taking its principal melody from no. 9, here with a more solid form of imitation and between a larger number of voices, the soldiers' derisive chorus, "Greetings, dear King of the Jews!", likewise conveys dramatic irony to Christians, who would say that Jesus *is* in fact the king, not only of "the Jews" but of all humanity, and who would also say that proper discipleship is tied up with recognizing his status as the Divine King. At this point in the passion narrative Jesus is about to "draw them all" to himself by means of the cross (see the language of no. 9, *höre nicht auf, selbst an mir zu ziehen,* "do not cease, yourself, to pull at me"[42]). Bach's music projects the view that the ability to follow Jesus comes from *him* as divine ruler, drawing people to him by his crucifixion, and that discipleship is not ultimately a decision *you* make. This conforms to the standard Lutheran teaching that Christian belief is a gracious and undeserved gift from God, and that there is no justification before God by human good works.

Bach's setting brilliantly expresses this notion of faith and discipleship for Peter's denials of Jesus. Peter's first words in the *St. John Passion* come at no. 10 when the doorkeeper of the high priest's palace asks him, "Are you not one of [Jesus'] disciples?" Peter answers, *Ich bin's nicht* ("I am not"). His denial comes in G major in a way that calls to mind the V–I cadence in G of Jesus' I AM (Ex. 11: Kuijken, CD 1, track 13, 0:43–0:56); but where Jesus' G major melody was simple and its harmony straightforward, Peter's version is heavily ornamented and its harmony is more convoluted. In other

---

42. This is the language of John's gospel. In John 12:32, Jesus is depicted as saying, "when I am lifted up from the earth [Calov, *Die heilige Bibel,* V, 845–46: "on the cross's beam / John 3:14" — identical comment in Olearius, *Biblische Erklärung,* V, 718], I shall draw them all to myself [i.e., effect redemption — *so wil ich sie alle zu mir ziehen;* Calov, *Die heilige Bibel,* V, 846, adds: "through the Word of the gospel"]." Olearius (*Biblische Erklärung,* V, 718) refers to Jesus' *ziehen* here as "the spiritual magnet" and adds, "[this] power of the cross could even split the rocks and open the graves — Matthew 27" (cf. the interpolation from Matthew 27 at the recitative no. 33). See also John 6:44, where Jesus says, "No one can come to me unless drawn by the Father [*es sei denn, daß ihn ziehe der Vater*] who sent me; and I will raise that person on the Last Day."

words, whereas Peter verbally denies Jesus, the ornamented music related to a simpler source could convey something else: not the banal fact that Peter is lying, but that his discipleship has not actually been called into question by his behavior.[43] True to Lutheran teaching, the validity of faith and discipleship depends upon God, not humans' good works. And it is of course only Jesus, as Son of God, who can say *Ich bin's*.

These ideas concerning faith and works are developed further, again musically, in the aria that follows Peter's third denial, *"Ach, mein Sinn"* (no. 13). This number was adapted from the first strophe of Christian Weise's poem *"Der weinende Petrus"* in *Der grünen Jugend*. Although Weise's poem was entitled "The Sobbing Peter," Peter himself does not sing this aria in the *St. John Passion,* presumably because others are meant to identify with his denials as fellow sinners.[44] Bach set Weise's words as a tenor aria (Peter is a bass in the *St. John Passion,* and although in this work one singer might play multiple characters, it appears from Bach's own performing parts that each character is always assigned to the same singer). The aria's words and their musical setting are especially tortured. Yet the underlying rhythm often follows the sarabande, the noblest and most advanced of the French court dances that were cultivated also by Leipzig burghers in Bach's day[45] (Ex. 13: Kuijken, CD 1, track 18, 0:29–0:43; in sarabandes, beats come in groups of three with clear secondary emphases on beat two).[46] Bach's music, it seems to me, conveys the message that all is not lost. The noble dance rhythms underlying the aria's tortured mood can be understood as God's Yes behind his No, Luther's way of expressing the paradoxical coexistence of God's condemning wrath and merciful grace.

It is through these two key numbers and a third aria that Bach's music can be seen to portray stages in maturing discipleship: eager innocence in

43. Much less easily noticed, Peter's ornamented version of the cadence formula also conforms to the shape of the closing words of no. 9, at the place where Jesus is affirmed as "my light," on scale degrees 5 up to 3 over V, down to 2 and 1 over I (Ex. 12: Kuijken, CD 1, track 12, 3:36–3:42). My thanks to Danielle Tylke for this observation. Peter's second denial, at no. 12c, will be set to the same pattern but one step higher, with A as the home pitch.

44. Dürr, *Johannes-Passion,* 49, n. 4. In this transfer of voice from Peter to an "existential I," everyone is being petrified, as it were (my thanks to John Butt for this formulation). In contemporary passion sermons, too, Peter is taken for the Protestant Christian as an example of the remorseful sinner with whom one is to identify (Steiger, "Wo soll ich," 39–40).

45. Little, *Dance and the Music of J. S. Bach,* 9–14, 94.

46. *"Ach, mein Sinn"* is identified with sarabandes also in Finke-Hecklinger, *Tanzcharaktere in Johann Sebastian Bachs Vokalmusik,* 23, 62–63, 139, 141. This is not to say, however, that the aria ought to be rendered in sarabande tempo. For an example of Bach's writing in sarabande rhythms but obscuring them by specifying an "incorrect" tempo, in this case too slow, see the second movement of his Sonata in G minor for obbligato harpsichord and viola da gamba (BWV 1029); Dreyfus, "J. S. Bach and the Status of Genre," 64–70.

"Ich folge dir gleichfalls" (no. 9), recognition of sin and confession in *"Ach, mein Sinn"* (no. 13), and the taking up of the cross in *"Eilt, ihr angefochtnen Seelen"* (no. 24), which answers the "where?" questions of no. 13 with "to Golgotha."[47] This leads to the question of how Jesus' glory and majesty are made manifest: in the cross.

Theology of the Cross

The gospel of John mentions Jesus' "drawing humanity to himself"[48] along with his glorification by God the Father. It may seem strange that the evidence for Jesus' being a majestic king is located in the lowliness of the cross. Lutheranism, however, is largely defined by this idea of glorification through abasement, and Bach's music projects its sense profoundly. According to Luther, one finds God "hidden in opposites." The central place for locating one's faith in God is at the cross, and humans find God's glory *only* there. Related to this is Luther's belief in God's "alien" versus "proper" work, according to which people are "struck down" by God, like Jesus was, in order that they may be "raised up" to redemption. What we see around us is misery, but this can be taken as a sign that God is with us and that peace and happiness will be ours (alien work logically precedes proper). This is what the theology of the cross is all about. Luther's theology posits faith. Faith is confidence in what is unseen, and faith appears to be, as Luther often put it, "in opposition to experience." The theology of the cross is meant to become a "model for one's life,"[49] in that one's suffering is to be taken as a sign not of God's abandonment but of his presence.

Bach's aria *"Es ist vollbracht"* (no. 30) projects Luther's theology of the cross most forcefully. At first it seems as though the notes simply contradict the words, since Jesus' cry of triumph[50] is set as a somber dirge. But these are surface features. The aria is scored with an obbligato for a special instrument, the viola da gamba, a favorite solo instrument in French Baroque court music; and often the underlying rhythms are the ones cultivated in the majestic style of Louis XIV's court music and therefore widely

47. Stapert, "Christus Victor," 22–23.
48. See n. 42 above.
49. Luther, "A Meditation," 13–14.
50. The word for *es ist vollbracht* ("it is accomplished") in the original Greek was *tetelestai,* a cry of triumph, something that is obscured in the common English rendering "it is finished." Olearius (*Biblische Erklärung,* V, 788) mentions that the Greek here reads *tetelestai,* and he goes on to say this involves "triumph . . . and the joyous resurrection of our redeemer, Job 19 [vs. 25] . . . so it is expressed, accordingly: 'the battle is accomplished [*vollbracht*], the victory is secured,' *NB Vici,* John 16:33, *Victoria,* 1 Corinthians 15:57, 'now have I conquered.'"

imitated elsewhere: continually alternating long and short values in a ratio of about three to one, notated with dots next to the longer note values and thus called the "dotted style" (see Bach's *"Contrapunctus 6 . . . in Stylo Francese"* from the *Art of Fugue*). The aria is marked *molto adagio* (very leisurely, slow[51]), however, and the notes are mostly slurred (connected together smoothly rather than separately articulated). Thus although it is notated in the dotted style, this gamba music, owing to its slowness and smoothness, sounds sombre. That is to say, only on the page, which listeners do not see, does the music appear majestic. As Bach's music has it, then, Jesus' majesty is "hidden" in its opposite, which is very much a Lutheran approach (Ex. 14: Kuijken, CD 2, track 26, 0:00–1:31).

The middle section of this aria is set in the tradition of Monteverdi's *stile concitato* (fast repeated notes, an Italian Baroque convention for "militant" affects). This is more what one would expect from a victorious Christ (Ex. 15: Kuijken, CD 2, track 26, 3:46–4:42). But the final notes spell a diminished chord, the most unstable harmony available in Bach's vocabulary. This middle section cannot stand formally closed (contradicting the sentiment of the libretto's *schließt*) as in conventional Baroque arias. It has to resolve somehow, and it does so right into the slow gamba music of the opening section again (Ex. 16: Kuijken, CD 2, track 26, 4:38–5:13). The soloist now even shapes the *Es ist vollbracht* melody in exactly the same way that Jesus sang those words in the previous recitative (no. 29; Ex. 17: Kuijken, CD 2, track 25, 0:45–1:15). Hair-raisingly, the Jesus form of the melody is sung once again, superimposed on the final cadence of the aria[52] (Ex. 18: Kuijken, CD 2, track 26, 5:32–6:09).

These final words of Jesus were apparently important to Bach personally as well. In his Calov Bible, he underlined in the commentary the sentence where their full meaning for humanity is spelled out:[53] "Christ's Passion is the fulfillment of scripture and the accomplishment of salvation of humankind."[54] By Jesus' revealing who he is (the victorious Son of God) in a way that can be seen only by faith, people have been freed from sin. Unlike in the gospel of Matthew and Bach's *St. Matthew Passion*, one does not have to

---

51. In Bach's music, the slow end of the tempo continuum is generally represented by *adagio*, not *largo*; see Marshall, "Tempo and Dynamics," 266.

52. Arias conventionally close with the instruments alone restating their material from the introduction.

53. Scientific research has determined that the chemical content of the ink in the underlinings is the same as that of the marginal comments whose handwriting characteristics were identified with Bach's by Hans-Joachim Schulze of the Bach-Archiv, Leipzig (Kusko, "Proton Milloprobe Analysis," 31–106).

54. Calov, *Die heilige Bibel,* V, 947; Cox, *Calov Bible,* facs. 250.

wait until Jesus' resurrection for victory. In the Johannine view, victory is secured already at the cross.

Especially at no. 30, Bach's *St. John Passion* shows a deep grasp of this gospel's notion that the sum and substance of faith reside in recognizing Jesus' identity as God and king, and seeing in the cross the way his identity is essentially proclaimed. Jesus has a certain job to do, and it is possible for him to do his work of redemption only because of who he is.

Lutheran Concepts of Jews and Judaism

Having considered the less troubling sides of the *St. John Passion's* Lutheranism, let us continue exploring its central messages through a discussion of more disquieting aspects.

The Gospel of John

There is no general agreement today on whether or not the gospel of John, with its continual references to "the Jews," should be considered essentially anti-Judaic (condemning categorically the beliefs, practices, and practitioners of the religion of Judaism), or on whether or not it should be considered essentially antisemitic (condemning Jews as a people or "race," without necessarily being concerned about religious beliefs and practices, identifying individuals as "Jews" and attributing characteristics, agendas, and roles to them on that basis alone).[55] The issues of John's gospel are not necessarily identical to those of Bach's *St. John Passion,* which is mostly taken up with post-Reformation Lutheran poetic commentary (chorales and arias) on John's biblical narrative. That is to say, Bach's work is an extended musical commentary on and interpretation of John, and therefore familiarity with the gospel, though important and relevant, cannot substitute for study of

55. See Langmuir's remarkably insightful essay, "Toward a Definition of Antisemitism." He argues that if it is to have any historical explanatory power, use of the term "antisemitism" should be reserved for socially significant hostility involving the attribution of unreal characteristics to "Jews." I follow Langmuir's and others' usage of "antisemitism" rather than "anti-Semitism"; Langmuir, 16: "Since there is in fact no such thing as 'semitism,' save when referring to a language, the term is literally meaningless when applied to Jews, which is why I refuse to hyphenate 'antisemitism.'" On conflating diabolical images and ideas with "the Jew," see the definitive study by Joshua Trachtenberg, *The Devil and the Jews;* see also Schreckenberg, *The Jews in Christian Art.* For some further comments on John, see n. 12 in the Annotated Literal Translation. For a convenient summary on John's extreme hostility to Jews, see Pagels, *Origin of Satan,* 98–111.

Bach.[56] To put it another way: to interpret the *St. John Passion* properly, we need to concern ourselves primarily not with what John's gospel means but with what it apparently has been taken to mean in Bach's music. The questions are whether or not Bach's music buys into the gospel's hostility to Jews, and whether or not Bach's music appropriates Luther's polemics.

One of the most uncomfortable expressions from the gospel's narrative within the *St. John Passion* appears at no. 38, where Joseph of Arimathea, himself surely Jewish, is identified as "a disciple of Jesus, but secretly, for fear of the Jews." It remains a subject of fierce debate in biblical and religious studies whether anyone — in Jesus' own day or in the gospel-writing days several generations later — who believed in Jesus actually had anything to fear from Jews who did not. The gospel of John and works of art based on it have been interpreted and used in many ways, including ones that promote anti-Jewish thought and violent action. (This is not to say that the gospel, whose writers are widely but perhaps wrongly believed among biblical scholars to have been ethnically Jewish,[57] represents with its oftentimes extreme hostility to Jews a blanket condemnation of all Jews for all times; but it very well might.) Our subject being Bach's *St. John Passion,* I think we should focus first and foremost on how Bach and his librettist interpret and use John's gospel.[58]

56. It should perhaps be noted, too, that passion plays are fundamentally different from the *St. John Passion.* They add all sorts of story elements and new characters to the canonical gospels, often thereby projecting unambiguous and pronounced anti-Jewish sentiments (see Brown, *Death of the Messiah,* 1347, passim); there are also passion plays, however, that focus instead on Christians' collective guilt. Luther and his followers banned passion plays, and their performance continued only in the Catholic territories of Germany (the present-day Oberammergau passion play is a remnant of this latter tradition); see Holstein, *Reformation in Spiegelbilde,* 25, 31; Michael, "Luther and the Religious Drama," 365–67. In Bach's *St. John Passion,* we have a verbatim story from a sacred canon, something set with extensive commentary that has become part of an artistic canon. Passion plays are in neither a sacred nor an artistic canon. Because passion plays and Bach's music are put together in fundamentally different ways, because they have been received so differently, and because they are not actually related to each other historically, discussing passion plays is of extremely limited usefulness in explaining Bach's music or in determining how best or most responsibly to perform Bach's music. It has been my experience from giving lectures and participating in public forums that those who posit the relevance of passion plays have little or no familiarity with the plays or with Bach's music. For a helpful and well-informed treatment of passion plays, see Klenicki, *Passion Plays and Judaism.*

57. For arguments against Jewish authorship of John's gospel, see Fredriksen, *From Jesus to Christ,* 26 (my thanks to Frances Stier for this reference); cf. p. 226.

58. There are many references to Jews in Bach's Calov Bible Commentary, most of them neutral or negative. It may interest readers to know, although not too much should made of this, that Bach highlighted only one reference, a positive one. (Notice that one needs to compare facsimiles in Cox with their translations, as the latter often include surrounding material that was not actually highlighted by Bach.) At the commentary on Ecclesiastes 6:11, Bach highlighted the following passage (Cox, *Calov Bible,* 430):

The expression "the Jews" appears frequently in John's gospel,[59] usually with negative and other times with neutral, positive, or extremely positive connotations.[60] The phrase "for fear of the Jews," which can hardly be taken in any way but negatively, appears infrequently but in prominent and significant places (see 7:13, 19:38, and 20:19; compare 12:42). The scriptural source for the interpretive controversy surrounding this expression is John 9:22. The following most likely represents what the expression is taken to mean in the *St. John Passion,* the way John 9:22 reads in Bach's Calov Bible Commentary:

Therefore when wise people see that they often fail, even in the most useful matters of counsel, they do not let up, thinking always to themselves that if only we had acted differently, it would have turned out well. But one says, advice by hindsight is fool's advice, and the very acts of advice by hindsight which cost much and which one does not gain without personal harm are of no avail if God does not help. Of this we find numerous examples in the writings of the Gentiles and Jews, that kings, princes, and masters have not exceeded the measure set for them by God. However, the writings of the Jews differ from those of the Gentiles in that the Jews have received God's word and commandments and that they teach us through their writings that everything proceeds according to God's will and order, and for that reason these writings are all the more useful to read. For the Gentiles' writings are also great examples of God's justice, except that these instances occurred without God's direct bidding and command.

In writing the *St. John Passion,* Bach cannot have been well-acquainted personally with Jews, for Jews were then permitted in Leipzig only at its trade fairs (see Markgraf, *Zur Geschichte der Juden auf den Messen in Leipzig*). It is possible that he knew Christians from formerly Jewish families; Johann Abraham Birnbaum, who in the 1730s published a defence of Bach's music, may have been from such a family (Kreutzer, "Johann Sebastian Bach und das literarische Leipzig," 28, n. 55). It should not be assumed that a society without Jews is necessarily unlikely to foster anti-Jewish sentiment; consider, e.g., the endurance of anti-semitism in England from the fourteenth to the seventeenth centuries despite the absence of Jews (see Langmuir, *Toward a Definition of Antisemitism,* 45).

59. Although John's Greek could also in some instances appropriately be translated as "the Judaeans," Luther Bibles consistently use the expression *die Jüden* ("the Jews," as is the case in nearly all other translations; although the Judaeans were in any event Jews, an advantage in rendering John's term *hoi Ioudaioi* as "the Judaeans" would be that readers would be less likely to associate this group with today's Jews).

60. For the former, see, e.g., John 8:44, where Jesus is depicted as saying to Jews: "Your father is the devil and you choose to carry out your father's desires. He was a murderer from the beginning, and is not rooted in the truth . . ."; for the latter, see John 4:22: "Salvation comes from the Jews" (Calov, *Die heilige Bibel,* V, 747: *Das Heyl kömmet von den Jüden;* and the commentary adds, "[i.e.,] the saviour of the world; Romans 9:5"). Pro-Nazi Christians — I am not saying they were good Christians — in the Third Reich were of course unhappy with John 4:22. Theologians and pastors from the *Institute for the Study and Eradication of Jewish Influence on German Church Life,* for example, produced in 1940 a de-Judaized version of the New Testament, entitled *Die Botschaft Gottes* ("The Message of God"), in which all references to Jesus' Jewishness were eradicated; John 4:22 was changed to the famous anti-semitic slogan, "The Jews are our misfortune" (*die Juden sind unser Unglück*); see Heschel, "Nazifying Christian Theology," 595. Concerning whether or not John's gospel and Bach's music teaches that salvation comes *for* the Jews, see pp. 35–36 here.

Such things said his parents [of a blind man who had been healed by Jesus on a sabbath day] / because they were afraid of the Jews / (*of the leading men among the Jews / and of the Pharisees*) because the Jews had already agreed / if anyone acknowledged himself for [Jesus as] Christ / that he would be banned (*that he should be excommunicated / and regarded as a gentile*).[61]

Luther's Polemics

Luther had scathingly denounced as groups the Anabaptists, Jews, Muslims, and "Papists" (i.e., Roman Catholics), with much the same polemical language and with similarly harsh measures suggested for the first three of these groups. Only Luther's measures for Jews who would not embrace his Christianity are well-known today:[62] burn their places of worship (Luther actually goes so far as to claim that the Hebrew Scriptures support this), destroy their homes, seize their prayer books and Talmudic writings, and, since they refuse to change their ways (i.e., convert), expel them.[63] Convinced for a variety of reasons that the Last Days were imminent, Luther deemed it critical to avoid chaos and uphold the gospel against what he considered its disturbingly influential enemies, all four groups of whom, he claimed, placed a high redemptive value on good works. Luther had an extremely strong commitment to the idea that the Bible teaches salvation by grace through faith, not by works. He held that these groups needed to reach a point of praying for God's merciful bestowal of the gift of true faith[64] if they did not wish to incur damnation.[65] Contrary to what is sometimes asserted, Luther did not call for the extermination of the Jewish people — this would set at nought the eschatological plan of salvation believed to be attested in Romans 11, involving the notion that the conversion of the Jews to Christianity will be one of the events heralding the end of the world and the second coming of Jesus.[66]

---

61. Calov, *Die heilige Bibel,* V, 820 (regular type for John's gospel text, italics for Calov's commentary). For information on modern scholarly interpretation of John's expressions, see n. 32 in the Annotated Literal Translation. For Bach's settings of these sentiments of John's in his church cantatas *Sie werden euch in den Bann tun* (BWV 44 and 183), the "they" who ban and even kill God's people does not refer explicitly or implicitly to Jews but rather is explicitly spiritualized as part of the battle between God and the devil for the church and the Christian's soul.

62. Luther, "On the Jews and their Lies," 268–76.

63. See Hillerbrand, "Martin Luther and the Jews"; Edwards, *Luther's Last Battles;* and the extensive discussion in Oberman, *Roots of Anti-Semitism.*

64. Cf. Luther, "On the Jews and their Lies," 303.

65. See, e.g., Luther, "On the Jews and their Lies," 253, 268, 287.

66. See, e.g., Luther's scholia on Romans 11 in his *Lectures on Romans,* 429–31.

It is less widely known that in the post-Reformation period Lutheran passion sermons mostly dropped the polemics used specifically against these four religious groups and referred more generally to the "world" as the gospel's enemy.[67]

Luther's recommendations were repeated in Johannes Müller's *Judaismus,* a book that Bach also owned.[68] Renate Steiger contends that "in Bach's musical preaching this [Luther's and Müller's] polemic played . . . no role."[69] The question, I would argue, is not whether Bach himself was familiar with anti-Jewish polemics but whether his music projects or assumes them.

Luther and Hitler

Luther's extremely ugly pronouncements are probably wrongly construed as "racial" theories. Any Turk or Jew who embraced Luther's type of Christianity was to be supported as a fellow brother or sister in Christ: Luther said the assets of Jews who would not convert should be confiscated and used in no other way but to support those Jews who did sincerely convert.[70] Luther's ravings about the Jews, horrifying as they are, have perhaps too frequently and casually been dubbed the first works of modern antisemitism, a small step to Hitler, and the like.[71] This can easily thwart consideration of our reception of the post-Reformation Lutheranism of Bach's music.

67. Axmacher, *"Aus Liebe will mein Heiland Sterben,"* 88. There are, however, prominent exceptions. Probably the most rabid anti-Jewish remarks come from the pen of Erdmann Neumeister (1671–1756), an orthodox Lutheran pastor in Hamburg; see Wallmann, "Reception of Luther's Writings on the Jews," 84. Bach set several cantata texts by Neumeister, none of which refers to Jews or Judaism.

68. Hoffmann-Axthelm, "Bach und die *perfidia Iudaica,"* 43–45; see also the annotation for Müller, *Judaismus* in the list of Works Cited.

69. Steiger, "Bach und Israel," 22.

70. Luther, "On the Jews and their Lies," 270. In Lutheran theology, forced conversions were not conversions at all (see Müller, *Judaismus,* 1403). A closer contemporary antecedent for modern "racial" antisemitism can be found in the Pure Blood Laws (directed at New Christians, who were from formerly Jewish families) under Catholicism's Spanish Inquisition; see Friedman, "Antisemitism," 54–55, and Netanyahu, *Origins of the Inquisition.*

71. Carter Lindberg cites several prominent examples of that sort of matching of Luther and Hitler ("Tainted Greatness: Luther's Attitudes toward Judaism and Their Historical Reception," 15, 30; for other examples, see also Wiener, *Martin Luther: Hitler's Spiritual Ancestor,* 68–79, passim): Julius Streicher, the Third Reich's *Judenfresser* ("devourer of the Jews"), defended himself on the charge of genocide at the Nuremberg Trials by appealing to Luther, noting that "Dr. Martin Luther would be sitting in my place. . . . [In] 'The Jews and Their Lies' [he] wrote the Jews are a brood of snakes, one should burn down their synagogues, one should annihilate them"; the great German philosopher Karl Jaspers later echoed these sentiments, declaring "There [Luther states] already the entire program of the Hitler

Luther on Jews as "Christ Killers"

Lutheran theology's anti-Judaism did not incorporate the long-sanctioned condemnation of Jews as *the* "Christ killers." While Luther certainly thought Jews were guilty in Jesus' crucifixion,[72] neither he nor his followers believed that Jews alone, or even primarily, were accountable. The historical Romans and later Christians, and indeed all people, were also considered guilty, as will be explained later in the present discussion. The traditional Christ-killer sentiments are certainly found readily in dictionaries and secular songs of Bach's day.[73] There is nothing of that sort, however, in the standard Lutheran theology textbook read by Bach as a young student[74] and

---

era!" (cf. Shirer, *Rise and Fall of the Third Reich*, 236); and Alan Dershowitz recently reiterated the charges, concluding that "It is shocking that Luther's ignoble name is still honored rather than forever cursed by mainstream Protestant churches. The continued honoring of Luther conveys a dangerous message, a message that was not lost on Hitler: namely, that a person's other accomplishments will earn him a position of respect in history, even if he has called for the destruction of world Jewry" (Dershowitz, *Chutzpah,* 107). In his second sentence Dershowitz identifies a genuine problem; one might question only whether in his equating Luther's and Hitler's hostility to Jews he has accurately historicized it. It is evident from reading Luther's writings that he had not recommended, and could not have supported, the extermination of the Jewish people envisaged by the Nazis and their supporters, although his attitudes are ones that cannot ever be tolerated. Luther was consistently dismissive of the religious beliefs and practices of Judaism, and while he eventually gave up hope that significant numbers of Jews would come around to his way of seeing things, he remained concerned to his last sermon that there might still be among them a few of what he called *true Israelites* (potential believers in his sort of Christianity). What was new in Luther's later writings was that he ascribed to Jews who would not convert the traditional medieval chimerical fantasies: ritual murder of Christian children, well-poisoning, and the like. In this context Luther chillingly goes so far as to say, "we are at fault in not slaying them" ("On the Jews and their Lies," 267). To sum up bluntly, then, if Luther's worldly ideal was a newly imagined *corpus Christianum* (universally Christian society) free of adherence to the religion of Judaism, Hitler's was a German Reich "racially" free of Jews. The alleged equivalence of Luther's and Hitler's hostility to Jews was questioned with great forcefulness in Gordon Rupp's monograph of 1945, *Martin Luther: Hitler's Cause — or Cure?* He notes (at p. 84): "I suppose Hitler never read a page by Luther. The fact that he and other Nazis claimed Luther on their side proves no more than the fact that they also numbered Almighty God among their supporters." Luther's figure has loomed so large that one can of course posit Luther's influence even on those who have not read a word of his. The point Rupp raises is, rather, what *did* Luther say? Franklin Sherman (Klenicki and Sherman, "Luther and Lutheranism on the Jews and Judaism," 16) comments on these matters: "clearly . . . [there are] historical connections between Luther's anti-Judaism and what happened later in the Holocaust — not in the sense of a simple cause-and-effect relation, but in the sense of its being a contributory factor. Of course, this should not be exaggerated — [having noted that several countries where the Lutheran church was dominant had a fine record in safeguarding Jews from the Nazis,] let's remember that Hitler himself was an Austrian Catholic."

72. Luther, "On the Jews and their Lies," 215, 226, 232, 261–63, 299.

73. Geck, *Johannespassion,* 84–85.

74. Hutter, *Compend of Lutheran Theology,* 2–242.

which was still used in the St. Thomas School of Leipzig during his tenure there.[75] That is to say, Bach's music may have been influenced more by Lutheran teaching on this issue than by the popular culture of his time.

In his passion sermon of 1519,[76] Luther writes, "You [each Protestant Christian churchgoer] should be terrified . . . by the meditation on Christ's passion. For the evildoers, the Jews, whom God has judged and driven out, were only the servants of your sin; you are actually the one who, as we said, by his sin killed and crucified God's Son."[77] In his sermons on John's passion narrative, Luther writes, "Now whoever wants to read Christ's suffering properly should not be angry with Judas and the Jews but rather look upon this person, the one who says 'Ich bins.'"[78] The Wittenberg hymnal of 1544 contains the following stanzas, now securely attributed to Luther:

Unser grosse sunde und schwere missethat	Our great sin and sore misdeed
Jhesum, den waren Gottes Son ans Creutz geschlagen hat.	Jesus, the true Son of God, to the cross has nailed.
Drumb wir dich, armer Juda, darzu der Jüden schar,	Thus you, poor Judas, as well as the host of Jews,
Nicht feintlich dürffen schelten, die schult ist unser zwar.	we may not inimically upbraid; guilt is truly ours.
Kirieleison.	Lord, have mercy.
Gelobet seist du, Christe, der du am Creutze hingst	Praise be to you, Christ, you who on the cross did hang
und vor unser Sunde viel schmach und Streich empfingst,	and for our sin many indignities and blows accepted,
jtzt herschest mit dem Vater in dem Himelreich;	[and who] now reigns with the Father in the kingdom of heaven;
mach uns alle selig auff diesem erdreich.	make all of us in this earthly realm blessed.
Kirieleison.	Lord, have mercy.[79]

---

75. Stiller, *Johann Sebastian Bach and Liturgical Life,* 175.

76. Reprinted in his *Church Postil* and widely circulated and studied into Bach's day (Axmacher, *"Aus Liebe will mein Heiland Sterben,"* 11–27). Chafe, *Tonal Allegory,* 134–40, argues that Bach's church cantata *Weinen, Klagen, Sorgen, Zagen* (BWV 12) follows the outlines of Luther's 1519 passion sermon.

77. Luther, "A Meditation," 10.

78. Luther, *Das 18. und 19. Kapitel,* 233; he makes negative comments about Jews at pp. 267, 376–77.

79. Luther, *Luthers Geistliche,* 313–14; the first stanza is quoted in Oberman, *Roots of Anti-Semitism,* 136, n. 120; cf. Axmacher, *"Aus Liebe will mein Heiland Sterben,"* 59–60, 113–14. What I have provided here is a literal translation, not one that could be sung comfortably.

Luther had adapted the first stanza from the medieval *Judasstrophe* that read:

O du armer Judas, was hast du getan,	O you poor Judas, what have you done,
daß du deinen Herren also verraten hast!	that you your Lord have so betrayed!
Darum mußt du leiden in der Hölle Pein;	Therefore you must suffer pain in hell;
Lucifers Geselle mußt du ewig sein.	Lucifer's companion you must be forever.
Kyrie eleison.	Lord, have mercy.[80]

In his *Hauspostille* of 1544, concerning Jesus' prayer for the Romans and Jews, "Father forgive them, for they know not what they do" (Luke 23:34), Luther writes, "when he prays for those who crucify him, he prays for us, the 'we' who with our sins give the reason for his cross and dying."[81]

Heiko Oberman puts matters in perspective in the following way:

[S]olidarity in sin between "us wretched Christians"[82] and the Jews loses its penitential and reformatory force if "Reformation" is understood as having already led true Christians out of the bondage of ecclesiastical despots, the final Babylonian captivity before the end. Such Protestant triumphalism permits heretics, papists, Jews, and "us wicked Christians" to be looked back upon as past history. Then the "Jewish probe,"[83] prophetic gauge in the service of the Reformation struggle for the Church at the beginning of the end,[84] is no longer safe from exploitation as a racist final solution.[85] Through the Jews Martin Luther unmasked the capability of Christians to ally themselves with the primeval enemy of Heaven and earth.[86] Eliminating this shocking view of Christians results in a destructive view of the Jews. Once this fundamental theological structure has collapsed, the [theological] anti-Judaism found in Luther — as in the Christian faith as a whole — becomes a pawn of modern ["racial"] anti-Semitism.[87]

80. Printed in Luther, *Luthers Geistliche,* 123.

81. Cited in Steiger, "Bach und Israel," 20–21.

82. This is what early Protestants were called.

83. That is, the seeking out of Jews, in the sixteenth century, for conversion (and in the mid-twentieth, for extermination).

84. That is, as mentioned earlier, Luther and his sixteenth-century followers believed they were living in the Last Days.

85. *Endlösung* ("final solution") was the Nazi term for effecting a *Judenrein* or *Judenfrei* ("Jew-free") world.

86. That is, the devil.

87. Oberman, *Luther,* 297.

Jew-Hatred and the *St. John Passion*

Olearius and Brockes

The *St. John Passion* was written with the understanding that Jesus and his immediate disciples ("the twelve") and subsequent followers, including, as Olearius likewise mentions, the gospel writer,[88] were Jews. Jesus is identified as a Jew, positively and powerfully, in Bach's aria *"Es ist vollbracht,"* no. 30.[89]

Bach's libretto borrows liberally from various contemporary German passion settings for the arias,[90] and, so far as I know, no previous writer has pointed out that its versions of some of these commentary verses do not contain the egregiously anti-Jewish remarks found in their well-known source. I am referring to the *Brockes-Passion* from the 1710s, *Der für die Sünde der Welt gemarterte und Sterbende Jesus,* set for nonliturgical performances by the leading German composers except Bach and which was frequently at the time even read just as a poem.[91]

The poetry in Bach's no. 19 is closely based on *"Drum, Seele, schau mit ängstlichem Vergnügen"* from the *Brockes-Passion.* The last line of Bach's version is not found in Brockes. Bach's line appears in the place of the second half of Brockes's number, which begins, "Look how his murderers [*Mörder*] plough his back, how deep, how cruelly deep they cut their ridges. . . ." Brockes set the entire passion narrative as his own poetry (a non-liturgical genre called the passion oratorio), rather than quoting the gospels' prose verbatim and featuring poetry only as inserted commentary on the gospel (as is the case in Bach's *St. John Passion,* a liturgical genre called the oratorio passion). Within Brockes's continuously poetic version, soldiers (*Kriegsknechte*) are identified as Jews whom Jesus had taught in the synagogue, and soldiers are the ones who cut Jesus' back. In the biblical text within Bach's *St. John Passion,* this brutal action is attributed to Pilate (at no. 18c).[92]

---

88. Olearius, *Biblische Erklärung,* V, 591.

89. The same is true of Bach's *Easter Oratorio* (BWV 249) and his church cantatas *Nun komm, der Heiden Heiland* (BWV 62), *Wo Gott der Herr nicht bei uns hält* (BWV 178), and *Erwünschtes Freudenlicht* (BWV 184). The expression *Held aus Juda* ("hero from Judah") stems from Luther's translation of Genesis 49:10 (cf. Revelation 5:5). John 4:9 (cf. 4:20–22) also identifies Jesus as a Jew.

90. Dürr, *Johannes-Passion,* 56–64.

91. Axmacher, *"Aus Liebe will mein Heiland Sterben,"* 116.

92. Luther, *Das 18. und 19. Kapitel,* 338, comments on Jesus' scourging by Pilate: "Pilate is a heathen and a thorough bloodhound." There are also other non-liturgical vocal works in which Jesus' scourging is attributed, unbiblically, to "the Jews"; see, for example, the setting of the secular passion carol "Woefully arrayed" by William Cornysh (d. 1523), whose first verse includes the lines: "Unkindly entreated, with sharp cord sore fretted, the Jews me

Luther Bibles do not identify Jews as *Kriegsknechte* (official army soldiers — literally, "war servants," something Jews by definition would not have had in a province like Judaea that was under Roman rule).[93]

The poetry in Bach's no. 24 derives from *"Eilt, ihr angefochtne Seelen"* in the *Brockes-Passion.* The second line in Brockes, however, is concerned not with Bach's fellow Christians leaving inner spiritual turmoil for the peace of the cross, but with the Jews in the narrative "leaving Achshaph's dens of murder." Achshaph was one of the many cities the Israelites, under Joshua, are depicted as having destroyed in their battles to take over the Promised Land of Canaan. "Leaving none that breathed" (Joshua 11:11), the Israelites burned Canaan's cities to the ground, except for those that stood on Canaan's hills (11:12–13). Brockes's apparent moral: "old Israel" should leave its murderous depths behind and fly to the hilltop of Calvary.

Here, in tabular form, is a comparison, with literal translations, of Handel's and Bach's versions of Brockes's aria (crossed-out words are from Handel's version, italicized words from Bach's):[94]

Eilt, ihr angefochtnen Seelen,	Hurry, you besieged souls,
Geht aus ~~Achsaphs~~ *euren* ~~Mörderhöhlen~~ *Marterhöhlen,*	leave ~~Achshaph's~~ *your* ~~dens of murder~~ *dens of torment,*
~~Kommt~~ *Eilt* — Wohin? — nach Golgatha!	~~come~~ *hurry* — where? — to Golgotha!
~~Eilet auf~~ *Nehmet an* des Glaubens Flügel,	~~Hurry towards~~ *Embrace* faith's wings;
~~Fliegt~~ *Flieht* — Wohin? — zum ~~Schädelhügel~~ *Kreuzeshügel,*	~~fly~~ *flee* — where? — to the ~~skulls'~~ ~~hilltop~~ *cross's hilltop,*
Eure Wohlfahrt ~~blühet da~~ *blüht allda!*	your welfare blossoms there![95]

Bach and a student copied out a score of Handel's setting of the *Brockes-Passion* in the 1740s, but there is no evidence that Bach put on the work

---

threatened. / They mowed, they grinned, / they scorned me. Condemned to death, / as thou mayest see, / Woefully arrayed."

93. The *strategoi* ("captains of the Temple"), mentioned only in Luke-Acts (Luke 22:4, 22:52, Acts 4:1–3, 5:21–24, 5:26; Brown, *Death of the Messiah*, 1430–31), who have limited policing prerogatives, are always translated by Luther as *Häuptleuten* (plural) and *Häuptman* (singular).

94. See also the comments on this poem at n. 57 in the Annotated Literal Translation.

95. There is no difference in meaning between *blühet da* and *blüht allda.* The last word of Bach's version of the aria, however, now points to the first word of the biblical narrative that directly follows (at no. 25a): "there they crucified him" — *Allda kreuzigten sie ihn,* the only other occurrence of the word *allda* in the *St. John Passion.* This could suggest, but not of course prove, that the (uniquely transmitted) alterations to Brockes's poetry were made for the *St. John Passion* instead of a now lost source from which Bach's libretto was copied.

liturgically.[96] Also in the 1740s, not based on the score just mentioned, Bach employed several of Handel's *Brockes-Passion* arias, including *"Eilt, ihr angefochtne Seelen,"* within a liturgical rendering of Reinhard Keiser's *St. Mark Passion.*[97] But since only the keyboard part survives, we do not know whether this time the words were the same as Handel's.

Musical Repetition and Symmetry

Another issue of some importance in interpreting the *St. John Passion* concerns Bach's fairly extensive reuse of the choruses on verbatim biblical texts. Attentive listeners may gather, or at least sense generally, that some of the repetitions result in an extended chiasmus, a figure arranged so that the order of events in one of two parallel series is inverted in the other (discussed further at p. 33). Choruses 23f/25b and 18b/21b are grouped at the edges, 23d and 21d are next in, and 23b and 21f are at the middle.

Dagmar Hoffmann-Axthelm sees this symmetry as part of the "biblically sanctioned and thus religiously constituted, Luther-bolstered and textually and musically integrated hostility towards Jews" of Bach's passion settings.[98] She explains that the repetitions express the blindness, stubbornness, and impenitence of the Jews, whereas the chorales express the suffering, love, and honor of Jesus and his followers.[99]

(I wonder if the *St. John Passion* readily lends itself to anti-Jewish construal because of the highly expert musical settings of the biblical choruses. No matter what the *St. John Passion*'s arias, chorales, and framing choruses may have to offer as commentary, what may still ring too easily in people's ears today are the terrifying repetitions of the biblical text's "Crucify, crucify!" If Bach's biblical choruses portray with great intensity the way some Jews reacted to Jesus, does this mean that the *St. John Passion* in part or *in toto* projects a universal hatred or negative view of the Jewish people?)[100]

---

96. Beißwenger (*Johann Sebastian Bachs Notenbibliothek,* 88) notes that Bach's score does not give the necessary indication of where the work would be divided into parts preceding and following the sermon. Furthermore, poetic versions of the passion narrative (such as Brockes's, as opposed to verbatim biblical versions) were simply not rendered in church services (Dürr, *Johannes-Passion,* 144–45). There are also no obvious venues for a non-liturgical performance in Leipzig in 1748/49 (when the copying of Bach's score was completed).

97. Beißwenger, *Johann Sebastian Bachs Notenbibliothek,* 178–83.

98. Hoffmann-Axthelm, "Bach und die *perfidia Iudaica,*" 33.

99. Hoffmann-Axthelm, "Bach und die *perfidia Iudaica,*" 46–53. A nearly identical interpretation was suggested by Pirro, *J. S. Bach,* 156; 171, n. 2.

100. See also n. 7 and n. 12 in the Annotated Literal Translation, which cite literature addressing the question of whether Jews were involved at all in seeking Jesus' death.

Hoffmann-Axthelm considers the center of the symmetry of repeated choruses to be the most striking, as in her view it involves dry, strict fugal form and awkward lining up of words and notes. As one of the very few studies to take up questions of anti-Judaism and Bach's music,[101] Hoffmann-Axthelm's article deserves more attention than it has received in the Bach literature. But it seems to me that there are some serious faults in her assessment of the *St. John Passion*.

It is true, for example, that contemporary writers on music sometimes refer to fugue as a useful procedure to express obstinacy. But consider Bach's procedure for nos. 21f and 23b. This fugue's theme, with its major scale and the off-beat accent on its highest pitch, sounds rather the opposite of obstinate (Ex. 19: Kuijken, CD 2, track 6, 0:00–0:28). The form, too, is uncharacteristically loose. And, furthermore, because it does not close on the home pitch, the number sounds open-ended. This particular fugal movement is decidedly neither dry nor strict.[102] On the other hand, in some performances, this fugue theme's off-beat accent can sound derisive.

101. Cf. Marissen, "Religious Aims"; L. Steiger, "Wir haben keinen König"; R. Steiger, "Bach und Israel"; Walter, "Die Bibel, Bach, die Juden."

102. Hoffmann-Axthelm, "Bach und die *perfidia Iudaica*," 50, goes on to say that this "rigid fugue-prison [nos. 21f and 23b] of the Jewish Law would be overcome by the New Song of the chorale [no. 22], at which (in the chorale) also the [Protestant Christian] listener would be symbolically present, taking from this opposition his moral: 'Through your imprisonment, Son of God, freedom must [*sic;* should be "has"] come to *us*.'" Hoffmann-Axthelm apparently takes the "us" (chorale-singing, freedom-possessed Christians) in the first line of no. 22 as contrasting with *them* (fugue-singing, legalistic Jews, to whom freedom cannot come). Throughout no. 22, it should be noted, *us* contrasts with *you* (Jesus): *your* imprisonment versus *our* freedom; *your* dungeon versus *our* refuge; *your* servitude versus *our* release from it. Hoffmann-Axthelm, 50, cites in support for her view the juxtaposition of old and new — i.e., the Old Law of Judaism and the New Song of Christianity — in Bach's *Actus tragicus*, the church cantata *Gottes Zeit ist die allerbeste Zeit* (BWV 106). I suspect this rests on a misinterpretation of the relationship between "law" and "gospel" in Lutheran theology (for a convenient introduction, see Westerholm, *Israel's Law and the Church's Faith*, 3–12; whether Luther properly interpreted the Bible on this issue is another question). In Lutheran teaching, God's law is not satisfied by outward fulfillment, since after the fall of Adam and Eve humans are essentially sinful, no matter what their actual behavior. The function of God's law is to make people feel its power, recognize their sin, experience God's wrath, and be led to repentance. The law, however, is not God's entire word. The gospel ("good news") stands alongside it. Law and gospel have opposite functions, even though both law and gospel contain aspects of the other. The law condemns and makes people conscious of their inherent sinfulness; the gospel preaches forgiveness of sins. The law places humans under the wrath of God; the gospel brings grace. According to Lutheran teaching, however, both the Old Testament and the New Testament contain elements of both law and gospel. It is this more nuanced view that Bach's Cantata 106 could more accurately be said to project. The fugue on "It is the old covenant: man, you must die" (Sirach 14:18) is rendered at the same time as the soprano solo "Yes come, Lord Jesus, come" (Revelation 22:20) along with an instrumental chorale. Old and new do not remain so distinct, however, for the fugue eventually takes on the melodic shape of the solo, and both are apparently derived from the melody of the

As will be shown later on, Hoffmann-Axthelm's characterization of the chorales is not quite accurate either. (Incidentally, she does not take note of the fact that there are chorale repetitions as well.) Furthermore, not only numbers sung by Jews but also ones by Roman soldiers[103] and by Christians are unsavory (e.g., in the 1750s, Friedrich Wilhelm Marpurg called such *wohin?* utterances as found in no. 24 "childish" and "brutish").[104] It cannot be entirely correct to say that Bach's choral repetitions serve to express the obstinacy of "the Jews" as a group if the repeated music is sung by varied sets of characters. Sometimes Bach's choruses depict only the chief priests, sometimes the chief priests with their attendants, sometimes "["the Jews"] all together," sometimes only the Roman soldiers — a situation that is obscured by Hoffmann-Axthelm's referring to Bach's repeated biblical-narrative choruses as *Juden-Turbae* ("Jew-crowds"; actually, neither the first-century Greek text of John's passion narrative, the standard Latin translation of it [the "Vulgate"], Luther's translation of the Greek, nor Bach's *St. John Passion* speaks of a Jewish "crowd"). All these sets of characters are considered to work against Jesus, but if a second set, or an overlapping but larger set, repeats (especially if only once) the music of a first set, how can Bach's music be said to express the obstinacy of the second?[105] (Not all listeners will pick up on these distinctions; if, however, they bunch the various sets together, they are, for whatever reason, misinterpreting the text.)

Hoffmann-Axthelm also points to the shameful practice, now abandoned, in medieval and later Roman Catholicism of praying for Jews as "obstinate" or "perfidious" in the prayers for Good Friday.[106] This was evidently not

---

well-known Lutheran chorale *Herzlich tut mich verlangen,* whose first stanza closes with the words "O Jesus, come soon" (see Dürr, *Die Kantaten von Johann Sebastian Bach,* 836–37). Thus in Cantata 106 grace is contained in law. On the connection of law with gospel, see also the alto recitative from Bach's church cantata *Bisher habt ihr nichts gebeten in meinem Namen* (BWV 87), whose third line reads, "You have deliberately transgressed law and gospel" (*Ihr habt Gesetz und Evangelium vorsätzlich übertreten*).

103. Terry (*Bach: The Passions,* 43–44) garbled his description, assuming the soldiers were Jews, when he pointed out that "there is subtlety in the association of the Jews' protest [no. 25b] with music that lately had expressed their derisory homage to the king of the Jews [no. 21b]."

104. Marpurg, *Anleitung zur Singekomposition,* 111–14; cited in Leisinger, "Forms and Functions of the Choral Movements in J. S. Bach's *St. Matthew Passion,*" 79–80.

105. Concerning the fact that, e.g., the similar choruses nos. 21b and 25b are sung by the Roman soldiers and the Jewish chief priests respectively, see Hoffmann-Axthelm, "Bach und die *perfidia Iudaica,*" 52, n. 75, where she suggests that both groups belong to the *Verstocktheits-Topos* (obstinacy topos) for Jews, familiar from the Middle Ages. Although there may be medieval iconography in which the soldiers have been depicted as "Jews," Lutheran interpretation of the passion narrative does not lump the Romans and Jews together in this way (see n. 6 in the Annotated Literal Translation). For Bach and his audience the soldiers were not Jews, nor were they depicted as "Jews."

106. Hoffmann-Axthelm, "Bach und die *perfidia Iudaica,*" 33–34.

the practice, however, in Lutheran services in early eighteenth-century Leipzig.[107] Their liturgical prayers for passion and Easter weeks have no such expression,[108] and their devotional prayers,[109] although they do refer to the "obstinate heart" (*verstocktes Hertz*)[110] and "blindness"[111] of the Protestant Christian, likewise make no explicit or implicit mention of Jews or Judaism.

The symmetry of choruses sung by the Roman soldiers and Jewish groups in the *St. John Passion* might better be understood to give formal expression to a Lutheran notion of the inevitability of Jesus' crucifixion, making it a reflection of God's predetermination — more fated, and less the result of a story that dynamically unfolds.[112] Its center may have been triggered by the biblical repetition of the words *Da Pilatus das Wort hörete* ("when Pilate heard those words") immediately following choruses 21f and 23b. Notice that there the evangelist's settings are melodically identical in the *St. John Passion*. There are obvious textual parallels between nos. 23d and 21d ("crucify") and between 25b and 21b ("King of the Jews"). Those between 18b and 23f concern replies to Pilate's either releasing or crucifying the "King of the Jews." The shape of the cross itself is symmetrical, as is Christ's name, symbolized by the Greek letter *X* (*chi*, from which comes the word "chiasmus"; notice the linking of "name" and "cross" in no. 26).[113] Recall, too, Bach's highlighting of the commentary on scriptural fulfillment at John 19:30 in his Calov Bible.[114] To put it succinctly, then, in some important respects the cross is both the form and the content of the *St. John Passion*.

107. Guides to these liturgies are found in Terry, *Joh. Seb. Bach: Cantata Texts,* and Stiller, *Johann Sebastian Bach and Liturgical Life.*

108. *Agenda: Das ist Kirchen-Ordnung,* 167–71.

109. *Leipziger Kirchen-Staat,* 194–211.

110. *Leipziger Kirchen-Staat,* 196.

111. *Leipziger Kirchen-Staat,* 207.

112. Cf. the symmetrical layout of Bach's *Christus victor* Easter cantata *Christ lag in Todesbanden* (BWV 4).

113. Each of the headings in the original sources for Bach's church cantatas for Advent (BWV 36, 61, 62, 132) reads "Adventus [or some abbreviation] Xsti." Pointing to Bach's use of the *X* symbol in his manuscripts of the *St. Matthew Passion* and church cantata *Ich will den Kreuzstab ["X-Stab "] gerne tragen* (BWV 56), Friedrich Smend ("Bach und Luther," 168) suggested that the choral symmetry in the *St. John Passion* was designed to represent the cross itself. (Hoffmann-Axthelm, "Bach und die *perfidia Iudaica*," 39, n. 26, cites Smend's essay in another connection but does not take note of its new interpretation of the symmetry in the *St. John Passion;* cf. Hoffmann-Axthelm, 47, n. 58.) Less interesting or (in my opinion) convincing is the sometimes encountered suggestion that the symmetry merely reflected time-saving measures on Bach's part. Rather more involved, musico-theoretical arguments have also been advanced for thinking of the entire *St. John Passion* as an enormous chiasmus (Chafe, *Tonal Allegory,* 275–335).

114. See the citation at n. 54 above.

Who Crucified Jesus?

To whom is accountability for Jesus' crucifixion attributed in the *St. John Passion?*

At no. 37, Bach's severe harmonies heighten the Christians' guilt sentiments of this Lutheran chorale (Ex. 20: Kuijken, CD 2, track 33, 0:00–1:16). To use technical language, the chorale is not in major or minor but in the Phrygian mode.[115] Its sentiments are echoed in the passion section of devotional prayers from a book used in Leipzig in Bach's day: "your [Jesus'] guiltless soul [has been brought] to the death. . . . Oh our sins, our heavy and great sins are the reason [*Ursach*]; because of them you were struck and tormented by God."[116]

The second stanza of no. 11 (Ex. 21: Kuijken, CD 1, track 14, 1:04–2:13), the Lutheran chorale with its remarkable dissonance on the first syllable of *Sünden* (sins), spells things out the most clearly and forcefully of all,[117] its "I, I" referring to the Lutheran congregants:

I, I and my sins,
which are as numerous as the grains
of sand on the seashore,
they have caused you
the sorrow that strikes you
and the grievous host of pain.[118]

Bach's *St. John Passion* proclaims next to no interest in the historical question "who killed Jesus?", whether it was Jews, Romans, or Jews and Romans together. It is concerned with theological questions about accountability for Jesus' death. Bach's efforts are predicated on the notion that, through the fall of Adam and Eve, all human beings (except Jesus) who have ever lived and ever will live are inherently sinful,[119] no matter what their actual behavior is. They are afflicted with what in theological terms is called "original sin." They are sinful by nature, for they have a "corrupted will"[120] — hence the Reformation contention that humans not only are sinners because they sin, but sin because they are sinners. In this view, all humans

115. Concerning the pitch content of the Phrygian mode, see n. 27 in the Annotated Literal Translation.

116. *Leipziger Kirchen-Staat*, 194.

117. See also nos. 13 and 20.

118. Another significant belief concerning the crucifixion, as expressed in nos. 4–5, is that it is God's will.

119. Protestant Christianity does not teach that Mary, the mother of Jesus, was also sinless.

120. The subject of humans' inheriting a "corrupted essence" (*verderbtes Wesen*) through "Adam's fall" is taken up extensively in Bach's church cantata *Erforsche mich, Gott, und erfahre mein Herz* (BWV 136).

are personally responsible for Jesus' death. Considered according to the tacit or acknowledged assumptions of other belief systems that do not subscribe to the Pauline-Augustinian-Lutheran conception of sin, the *St. John Passion* is virtually bound to be misinterpreted.

This is not to overlook the fact that there is projected in the *St. John Passion* some sense of a hierarchy of guilt. John's gospel story has Jesus saying to Pilate that whoever gave him over to the Roman authorities has "the greater sin" (see no. 21g). The *St. John Passion's* commentary, conforming to Lutheran teaching, strange though this may seem to much modern thinking, goes on to extend the levels of guilt in this hierarchy by placing Protestant Christians at the top (see especially nos. 11 and 37). Consider in this connection Luther's comments on John 19:11, where he says that "the Jews" are more evil and guilty than Pilate and the Roman soldiers,[121] and on John 18:38–40, where he says, after condemning Jews and Papists, "but because we [Protestant Christians] now [once again, truly] have Christ to preach, there have come on earth no more wicked people to be remembered than we."[122]

There is no hint in John's gospel that his followers of Jesus are to be considered more guilty of Jesus' crucifixion than Jews who reject Jesus, and in this respect we can see that the guilt issues expressed in the *St. John Passion* represent not only a significant departure from the passion settings of Bach's contemporaries but also a hermeneutical updating of the gospel itself.

Where Now?

From our vantage point it is certainly easy to see that Bach's setting by no means comes to terms with all ecumenically or socially troubling aspects of John's first-century text. For example, it does next to nothing to eliminate the sense that Judaism's understandings of the Torah have been entirely superseded by belief in Christianity's Jesus of Nazareth, the Son of God, as the only true path to God and redemption.[123] What is one to make of the

---

121. Luther, *Das 18. und 19. Kapitel,* 364–65; quoted in part in Calov, *Die heilige Bibel,* V, 936–37.

122. Luther, *Das 18. und 19. Kapitel,* 327; also John 19:19–22, where Luther says, "it is our sins that have placed him on the cross [*ligen im auff dem halse*]" (*Das 18. und 19. Kapitel,* 391; quoted *verbatim* in Calov, *Die heilige Bibel,* V, 944, except here for "sins" reading *Schulden,* not *Sünden*).

123. Jon D. Levenson, *Death and Resurrection,* v, sees a strange bond here between Judaism and Christianity: "[T]he longstanding claim of the Church that it *supersedes* the Jews in large measure continues the old narrative pattern [of the Hebrew Scriptures] in which a late-born son dislodges his first-born brothers, with varying degrees of success. Nowhere does Christianity betray its indebtedness to Judaism more than in its supersessionism."

commentary on John 19:30b at aria/chorale no. 32, where the aria asks concerning Jesus' death "is redemption of all the world [*aller Welt Erlösung*] here" and suggests that the answer is "yes"?[124]

I hope the present study is effective in suggesting that Bach's music could represent at least a step in the right direction, a step that might even prove helpful in today's continuing engagement with and defining of Christianity and its relationship to Judaism. Likewise, if thoughtfully organized performances of the *St. John Passion* can provide for some people the initial impetus for discussion not only of religious anti-Judaism but also of cultural, social, and political antisemitism, Bach's extended musical commentary on John's gospel may be able to help in accomplishing a sort of redemptive work that authentically builds on the gospel and Bach's music, yet at the same time moves forward from their original sectarian and liturgical purposes. In my view, this interpretive path could provide the ethically most intelligent way for attempting to reconcile historical and modern concerns.

In ongoing renderings of the *St. John Passion,* I hope it will be the more than thirty-fold repetition of the framing chorus's *Ruht wohl* (no. 39, "be fully at peace") that rings in people's ears.

---

124. The tension between the notions that all people are redeemed and that only some — God's "elect" — are redeemed is in fact a characteristic trait of John's gospel (Käsemann, *Testament of Jesus,* 62–65).

Annotated Literal Translation of the Libretto

But how shall men meditate in that which they cannot understand? How shall they understand that which is . . . in an unknown tongue? as it is written, "Except I know the power of the voice . . . he that speaketh shall be a Barbarian to me." (preface, King James Version of the English Bible, 1611)

The purpose of this translation is to present Bach's *St. John Passion* libretto in as close to a literal rendition of the German as is possible in American English (including some shifts from past to historical present tense that Luther took over from the New Testament's Greek). The style and syntax will therefore often leave a great deal to be desired. The translation is also designed to make as convenient as possible a line-by-line comparison of the German and English texts.

Luther's translation of the gospel of John's passion narrative[1] and mine of Luther's are printed in italics. Luther's text and, therefore, my translation do not necessarily correspond to any of today's English or German translations of the Bible.

The libretto's chorale responses to the biblical narrative are set in bold type, and the aria and arioso responses in regular type.

Many published translations of Bach's *St. John Passion* were designed to accommodate foreign-language renderings of the work (e.g., they focus on aligning syllabic with musical rhythms, particularly in the arias and chorales). For these and other reasons, such translations often substantially alter the meanings of the German libretto and thus hamper proper interpretation of the work.

The present translation's footnotes are designed to provide information that readers may wish to know about but which did not fit appropriately or smoothly into the main essay. They do not argue for or against the overall historicity of the gospel of John, a challenging subject on which there is a contradictory and overwhelmingly large bibliography. I have tried to indicate as best I could where the libretto is saying things whose historicity has been seriously called into question by subsequent scholarship, and where it is saying things whose historicity might reasonably but perhaps unjustly be

---

1. John 18–19, here with interpolations of Matthew 26:75 after John 18:27, and Matthew 27:51–52 after John 19:30.

doubted.[2] Full historical treatment and interpretation of the gospel would not, in any event, as suggested earlier (pp. 20–23), be entirely relevant to interpreting Bach's *St. John Passion.*

---

2. This is not meant to suggest that biblical interpretation gets better or worse over time. For a far-reaching philosophical critique of historical biblical scholarship, see Evans, *The Historical Christ and the Jesus of Faith,* 302–55. The main reason I have relied so heavily on Brown's book *The Death of the Messiah* is that it provides much more bibliographical and historical information in one place than does any other source. Regarding some well-known critics of Brown's methods and conclusions, see the annotation for his book in the list of Works Cited.

J. S. Bach, *Johannes-Passion*
  (BWV 245)

J. S. Bach, *St. John Passion*
  (BWV 245)

Parte prima

Part One

NR. 1 (1) CHOR
Herr, unser Herrscher, dessen Ruhm
In allen Landen herrlich ist!
  Zeig uns durch deine Passion,
  Daß du, der wahre Gottessohn,
  Zu aller Zeit,
  Auch in der größten Niedrigkeit,
  Verherrlicht worden bist!

NO. 1 (1)[3] CHORUS
Lord, our ruler, whose praise
is glorious in all the lands!
  Show us through your Passion
  that you, the true Son of God,
  at all times,
  even in the greatest abasement,
  have been glorified![4]

---

3. The first numbering listed will be that from the *St. John Passion* as edited by Mendel for the *Neue Bach-Ausgabe,* and the numbering in brackets from the first edition of Schmieder's *Bach-Werke-Verzeichnis.* Nearly all printed editions and recordings follow the numbering systems of one or the other of these sources.

4. This number is discussed in the main text, pp. 11–12, where *Ruhm* and *Herrlichkeit* are interpreted as "external glory" and "spiritual glory."

NR. 2a (2) REZITATIV
EVANGELIST
Jesus ging mit seinen Jüngern über den
Bach Kidron, da war ein Garte, darein
ging Jesus und seine Jünger. Judas aber,
der ihn verriet, wußte den Ort auch,
denn Jesus versammlete sich oft daselbst
mit seinen Jüngern. Da nun Judas zu
sich hatte genommen die Schar und der
Hohenpriester und Pharisäer Diener,
kommt er dahin mit Fackeln, Lampen
und mit Waffen. Als nun Jesus wußte
alles, was ihm begegnen sollte, ging er
hinaus und sprach zu ihnen:

NO. 2a (2) RECITATIVE
EVANGELIST
Jesus went with his disciples across the
brook Kidron,[5] where there was a
garden, which Jesus and his disciples
entered. Judas, however, who betrayed
him, also knew the spot, for Jesus often
gathered in that very place with his
disciples. Now when Judas had engaged
the band [of Roman soldiers][6] and
attendants of the chief priests and of the
Pharisees,[7] he comes to that place with
torches, lanterns, and with weapons.
Now since Jesus knew everything that
was supposed to happen to him, he
went out and exclaimed to them:

JESUS
Wen suchet ihr?

JESUS
Whom do you seek?

EVANGELIST
Sie antworteten ihm:

EVANGELIST
They answered him:

NR. 2b (3) CHOR
Jesum von Nazareth.

NO. 2b (3) CHORUS
Jesus of Nazareth.

5. Olearius's comments (*Biblische Erklärung*, V, 775) find echoes in the opening chorus: "Here goes the heavenly David, e.g., II Samuel 15:23, trailed by his disloyal son and disciple, in deepest abasement [*in tiefster Erniedrigung*]."

6. Luther's commentaries make clear that *die Schar* refers here to a band of Roman soldiers, not to a "crowd" or to "Jewish soldiers." Luther writes: "[Judas] takes two sorts of men with him, firstly, the Roman band [*Römer schar*], which consists of the governor Pilate's knights [*Reutter*] and servants; and secondly, attendants of the chief priests and of the Pharisees" (Luther, *Das 18. und 19. Kapitel*, 210; quoted in Calov, *Die heilige Bibel*, V, 913). See also Brown, *Death of the Messiah*, 248. Bach's audiences would presumably have been aware of this distinction from their pastors' sermons on the passion narrative, if not already from the setup of John's narrative itself (see n. 41 above).

7. After 70 C.E. ("Common Era"; a standard usage in place of A.D., "year of the Lord"), rabbis who followed the Pharisees' attitudes toward oral religious law were central to the Judaism known to the canonical gospel writers, and so these writers tend to give a similar prominence to the Pharisees in their stories about Jesus, sometimes for polemic reasons, sometimes by presumably unintended anachronism (Brown, *Death of the Messiah*, 1427). Recent historical research contends that there was no substantial conflict between Jesus and the Pharisees (Sanders, *Jesus and Judaism*, 270–93). Jesus was executed by the Romans, and if Jews did have anything to do with the crucifixion, it would have been at the instigation of those who had access to Pilate, principally the leaders of the priesthood (Sanders, *Jesus and Judaism*, 293). Other research argues that there was actually some serious opposition to Jesus from the Pharisees; see Saldarini, *Pharisees, Scribes and Sadducees*, passim.

NR. 2c (4) REZITATIV
EVANGELIST
Jesus spricht zu ihnen:

JESUS
Ich bin's.

EVANGELIST
Judas aber, der ihn verriet, stund auch bei ihnen. Als nun Jesus zu ihnen sprach: Ich bin's, wichen sie zurücke und fielen zu Boden. Da fragete er sie abermal:

JESUS
Wen suchet ihr?

EVANGELIST
Sie aber sprachen:

NR. 2d (5) CHOR
Jesum von Nazareth.

NR. 2e (6) REZITATIV
EVANGELIST
Jesus antwortete:

JESUS
Ich hab's euch gesagt, daß ich's sei, suchet ihr denn mich, so lasset diese gehen!

NR. 3 (7) CHORAL
O große Lieb, o Lieb ohn' alle Maße,

Die dich gebracht auf diese
    Marterstraße!
Ich lebte mit der Welt in Lust und
    Freuden,
Und du mußt leiden.

NO. 2c (4) RECITATIVE
EVANGELIST
Jesus exclaims to them:

JESUS
I am the one.

EVANGELIST
Judas, however, who betrayed him, also stood with them. Now since Jesus exclaimed to them, "I am the one," they drew back and fell to the ground.[8] He then asked them once more:

JESUS
Whom do you seek?

EVANGELIST
They again exclaimed:

NO. 2d (5) CHORUS
Jesus of Nazareth.

NO. 2e (6) RECITATIVE
EVANGELIST
Jesus answered:

JESUS
I have said to you that it is I; if you are in fact looking for me, then let these others go!

NO. 3 (7) CHORALE
O great love, O love beyond all
    measure,
that [has] brought you on this path
    of torment!
I lived with the world in delight and
    joy,
and you have to suffer.

8. The "absolute usage" of *ego eimi* ("I AM") is understood as an expression of divine self-revelation in the New Testament and in the Septuagint (the ancient Jewish Greek translation of the Torah and, eventually, the entire Hebrew Bible). The I AM utterances of the *St. John Passion* are discussed on pp. 13–15. (Whether Jesus actually made the self-claims he is depicted as having made in John's gospel is much debated in biblical scholarship.)

NR. 4 (8) REZITATIV
EVANGELIST
Auf daß das Wort erfüllet würde,
welches er sagte: Ich habe der keine
verloren, die du mir gegeben hast. Da
hatte Simon Petrus ein Schwert und zog
es aus und schlug nach des
Hohenpriesters Knecht und hieb ihm
sein recht Ohr ab; und der Knecht hieß
Malchus. Da sprach Jesus zu Petro:

JESUS
Stecke dein Schwert in die Scheide! Soll
ich den Kelch nicht trinken, den mir
mein Vater gegeben hat?

NR. 5 (9) CHORAL
Dein Will gescheh, Herr Gott,
   zugleich
Auf Erden wie im Himmelreich.

Gib uns Geduld in Leidenszeit,

Gehorsam sein in Lieb und Leid;
Wehr und steur allem Fleisch und
   Blut,
Das wider deinen Willen tut!

NO. 4 (8) RECITATIVE
EVANGELIST
In order that the Word would be
fulfilled, which he said,[9] *"I have not*
lost one of those whom you have given
me." Then Simon Peter had a sword
and drew it out and struck at the high
priest's servant and cut his right ear off;
and the servant's name was Malchus.
Then Jesus exclaimed to Peter:

JESUS
Put your sword in the scabbard! Shall I
not drink the cup that my Father has
given me?[10]

NO. 5 (9) CHORALE
Your will be done, Lord God, alike

on earth as [it is] in the kingdom of
   heaven.
Give us patience in time of
   suffering,
to be obedient in love and woe;
restrain and hold in check all flesh
   and blood
that acts against your will![11]

---

9. Jesus' own words in John 17:12.

10. In Matthew, Mark, and Luke's gospels, a distraught Jesus prays that God the Father might take away "the [metaphoric] cup." The gospel of John's Jesus, however, has no such hesitation about his crucifixion: let the Father's will be done and the Word be fulfilled. This is a key statement. Having already set the entire passage in recitative, Bach shifts the music to a melodious arioso and, uncharacteristically, has Jesus repeat his closing words (*den Kelch, den mir mein Vater gegeben hat?*). In the Hebrew Scriptures "the cup" symbolizes either joy and redemption or woe and suffering. Olearius, *Biblische Erklärung*, V, 777, considers John's gospel to be combining the symbols; he here cites Psalm 116:13 for the former and Psalm 75 [vs. 8] for the latter.

11. This chorale is placed specifically after Peter's action of resisting Jesus' arrest. Lutheran congregations recognize it immediately as one of the stanzas from Luther's chorale paraphrase of the Lord's Prayer, *"Vater unser im Himmelreich."*

NR. 6 (10) REZITATIV
EVANGELIST

Die Schar aber und der
Oberhauptmann und die Diener der
Jüden nahmen Jesum und bunden ihn
und führeten ihn aufs erste zu Hannas,
der war Kaiphas Schwäher, welcher des
Jahres Hoherpriester war. Es war aber
Kaiphas, der den Jüden riet, es wäre gut,
daß ein Mensch würde umbracht für
das Volk.

NO. 6 (10) RECITATIVE
EVANGELIST

The band, however, and the captain
and the attendants of the Jews took
Jesus and bound him and led him at
first to Annas (the father-in-law of
Caiaphas, the one who was high priest
in that year). But it was Caiaphas who
advised the Jews it would be good that
one man would be put to death for
[i.e., instead of] the people.[12]

12. See John 11:50, where Caiaphas says, "It is better for us that one man dies than the entire people be destroyed" (Calov, *Die heilige Bibel*, V, 839, with cross reference to John 18:14 and vice versa, V, 918; also Olearius, *Biblische Erklärung*, V, 778); on Caiaphas, see Horsley, "High Priests and the Politics of Roman Palestine," 35–37. Some consider it historically implausible that any Jew could ever have sought Jesus' crucifixion and that therefore already at this most basic level the passion narratives are antisemitic. One view — with some currency among the general public, I have discovered in giving lectures — is that the passion narrative was completely fabricated by the earliest gospel writer. A similar but more nuanced view is that the gospel writers for the most part imaginatively adapted imagery from Greek translations of the Hebrew scriptures that they took as their Bible. Agreeing that the canonical gospels are not modern, critical history books but suggesting that they are theological and artistic elaborations and interpretations of some events that probably did take place, a recent detailed survey of the literature argues for general historicity (Brown, *Death of the Messiah*, 328–97; see also n. 19 and n. 29 below in the present translation) and contends that John's is the least inaccurate account of Jewish interrogation proceedings (Brown, 363; cf. Sanders, *Jesus and Judaism*, 317–18). Another suggests that there were no trials at all (Crossan, *Who killed Jesus?*, 117), whereas yet another mentions that a "well-known passage in the Talmud [b. Sahn. 107b and parallel passages, b. Sotha 47a and j. Hag. 2.2, part of the Gemara on Sanh. 10.2] assumed that Jewish courts condemned and executed Jesus" (Pagels, *Origin of Satan*, 185, n. 8). (This is not to say that Jews do or should acknowledge responsibility for Jesus' death.) Cf. Brown, *Death of the Messiah*, 17, n. 23; and 376–77, where he discusses arguments for and against the idea that the Talmud's Yeshu is referring to Jesus of Nazareth, as well as observations on its possible dependence on the gospel of John. Much recent scholarship (e.g., the voluminous writings of Jacob Neusner) concludes that the Mishnah is often not helpful for understanding situations predating the Roman destruction of the Jerusalem Temple in 70 C.E. (Neusner, *Mishnah before 70*; concerning the proceedings at Jesus' trial, Neusner, *Mishnah: Introduction*, 150, n. 4; cf. Brown, *Death of the Messiah*, 346, 360; Sanders, *Jesus and Judaism*, 407, n. 16). The Mishnah is the first comprehensive book of Jewish law (it also contains other sorts of material), formulated around 200 C.E., which forms the foundation and constitution of Judaism as the basis for the two Talmuds: the Palestinian (Jerusalem) Talmud of around 450 C.E. and the Babylonian Talmud of around 500–600 C.E. On the great diversity of Judaisms in the land of Israel in ancient times, see Neusner, *Judaisms and Their Messiahs*.

NR. 7 (11) ARIE (ALT)
Von den Stricken meiner Sünden
Mich zu entbinden,
Wird mein Heil gebunden.
　　Mich von allen Lasterbeulen
　　Völlig zu heilen,
　　Läßt er sich verwunden.

NO. 7 (11) ARIA (ALTO)
From the ropes of my sins
to unbind me,[13]
my Salvation is bound.
　　From all my vice-boils
　　fully to heal me,
　　he lets himself be wounded.

NR. 8 (12) REZITATIV
EVANGELIST
*Simon Petrus aber folgete Jesu nach und
ein ander Jünger.*

NO. 8 (12) RECITATIVE
EVANGELIST
*Simon Peter, however, and another
disciple followed Jesus.*

NR. 9 (13) ARIE (SOPRAN)
Ich folge dir gleichfalls mit freudigen
　　Schritten
Und lasse dich nicht,
Mein Leben, mein Licht.
　　Befördre den Lauf
　　Und höre nicht auf,
　　Selbst an mir zu ziehen, zu
　　　　schieben, zu bitten.

NO. 9 (13) ARIA (SOPRANO)
I will follow you likewise with joyful
　　steps
and will not let you [go],[14]
my life, my light.
　　Hasten the way,
　　and do not cease,
　　yourself, to pull at, to push,
　　　　[and] to beseech me.[15]

NR. 10 (14) REZITATIV
EVANGELIST
*Derselbige Jünger war dem
Hohenpriester bekannt und ging mit
Jesu hinein in des Hohenpriesters Palast.
Petrus aber stund draußen für der Tür.
Da ging der andere Jünger, der dem
Hohenpriester bekannt war, hinaus und
redete mit der Türhüterin und führete
Petrum hinein. Da sprach die Magd,
die Türhüterin, zu Petro:*

NO. 10 (14) RECITATIVE
EVANGELIST
*This same disciple was known by the
high priest and went with Jesus into the
high priest's palace. Peter, however,
stood outside, in front of the door.
Then the other disciple, who was
known by the high priest, went out and
spoke with the woman keeping the door
and led Peter in. Then the maid, the
doorkeeper, exclaimed to Peter:*

MAGD
*Bist du nicht dieses Menschen Jünger
einer?*

MAID
Are you not one of this man's disciples?

13. Already in the instrumental introduction Bach's music marvelously captures the "bound - unbound" contrast. The oboes play dissonant notes that wind around each other and are tied over the bar line (in German, *Takt-Über*bindun*gen*) but which are followed by consonant ones in parallel motion. All of this sets up early in the passion the important theological theme of no. 22.

14. This is an allusion to Genesis 32:27, the story of Jacob's wrestling with God at Peniel. God says to Jacob, "Let me go" (*Laß mich gehen*), and Jacob answers, "I will not let you [go], unless you bless me" (*Ich lasse dich nicht* [*gehen*], *du segnest mich denn*).

15. This number is discussed on pp. 15–16.

EVANGELIST
Er sprach:

EVANGELIST
He exclaimed:

PETRUS
Ich bin's nicht.

PETER
I am not.

EVANGELIST
*Es stunden aber die Knechte und Diener
und hatten ein Kohlfeu'r gemacht (denn
es war kalt) und wärmeten sich. Petrus
aber stund bei ihnen und wärmete sich.
Aber der Hohepriester fragte Jesum um
seine Jünger und um seine Lehre. Jesus
antwortete ihm:*

EVANGELIST
*But the servants and attendants stood
around, having made a charcoal fire
(for it was cold), and warmed
themselves. But Peter stood among
them and warmed himself. But the
high priest asked Jesus about his
disciples and about his teaching.*[16] *Jesus
answered him:*

JESUS
*Ich habe frei, öffentlich geredet für der
Welt. Ich habe allezeit gelehret in der
Schule und in dem Tempel, da alle
Jüden zusammenkommen, und habe
nichts im Verborgnen geredt. Was
fragest du mich darum? Frage die
darum, die gehöret haben, was ich zu
ihnen geredet habe! Siehe, dieselbigen
wissen, was ich gesaget habe.*

JESUS
I have spoken freely and openly before[17]
*the world. I have always taught in the
synagogue and in the Temple, where all
Jews come together, and have spoken
nothing in secret. Why do you ask me
about this? About this, ask those who
have heard what I have spoken to
them! Behold, these same ones know
what I have said.*[18]

16. Olearius, *Biblische Erklärung*, V, 778: "[Jesus was asked about his teaching] to demonstrate that, as a false prophet and at the same time as a political agitator, he would be worthy of death (Deuteronomy 13:5)."

17. As is the case at several other spots in the libretto, the old form *für*, or *fur*, appears where today's German would use *vor*. (The libretto's usage of *vor* and *für* is not consistent.)

18. Jesus' words climb to ever higher pitches, with the highest on the *Ich* in the final sentence. The music also shifts its home pitch so that it closes with G as its tonal center. The final gesture is a merely instrumental V–I cadence in G. Bach's music, then, possibly projects the meaning of the last sentence as "Behold, these same ones know what I have said [namely: "I AM"]" (Ex. 22: Kuijken, CD 1, track 13, 1:34–2:22) — see the discussion of the theological significance of *Ich bin's* on pp. 13–15. The gospel of John's Jesus is quoting God's words from Isaiah 45:18–19 (my emphases), "For so speaks the Lord [who is] God; . . . *I am* [*Ich bin*] the Lord and there is no other. I *have not spoken in secret* [*habe nicht in verborgene geredet*]." Both passages are cross-referenced to each other in the Calov Bible Commentary (*Die heilige Bibel*, III, 258; V, 920). Olearius links the Isaiah passage and Exodus 3:14 to Psalm 27:1 (*Biblische Erklärung*, IV/1, 228).

EVANGELIST
*Als er aber solches redete, gab der Diener
einer, die dabeistunden, Jesu einen
Backenstreich und sprach:*

EVANGELIST
*But when he spoke such things, one of
the attendants who stood nearby gave
Jesus a blow to the face*[19] *and
exclaimed:*

DIENER
*Solltest du dem Hohenpriester also
antworten?*

ATTENDANT
Should you so answer the high priest?

EVANGELIST
Jesus aber antwortete:

EVANGELIST
But Jesus answered:

JESUS
*Hab ich übel geredt, so beweise es, daß
es böse sei, hab ich aber recht geredt, was
schlägest du mich?*

JESUS
*If I have spoken wickedly, then
demonstrate that it had been something
evil; but if I have spoken rightly, why
do you strike me?*

19. Olearius, *Biblische Erklärung*, V, 779, links this passage with Micah 5:1. Apparently such an action is historically plausible for the first century: Brown, *Death of the Messiah*, 585–86, cites Josephus, *War*, 6.5.3; #302, who reports that Jesus son of Ananias was arrested in the 60s C.E. by the leading citizens of Jerusalem because he stood in the Temple and prophesied destruction, at which, as he stood silent, they gave him many bruises, before they handed him over to the Romans. Crossan, *Who killed Jesus?*, passim, suggests that we should not, however, be concerned with what is plausible but with what our best guess is about what actually happened; is the gospel writing "history remembered" or "prophecy historicized"? (Crossan opts for the latter.) Another way of looking at the question of historical dependability would be to suggest that some details of the passion narrative are marked by such verisimilitude that they ought to be credited, whereas the palpably legendary and theological story elements should be identified as such; see Sloyan, *Crucifixion of Jesus*, 25. In some instances a fact may be "explained" in the canonical gospels by quoting the Hebrew Scriptures, not invented on the basis of them; see Sanders, *Jesus and Judaism*, 100. See also n. 12 and n. 29 in the present translation.

NR. 11 (15) CHORAL
Wer hat dich so geschlagen,
Mein Heil, und dich mit Plagen

So übel zugericht'?
Du bist ja nicht ein Sünder
Wie wir und unsre Kinder,
Von Missetaten weißt du nicht.

Ich, ich und meine Sünden,
Die sich wie Körnlein finden

Des Sandes an dem Meer,
Die haben dir erreget
Das Elend, das dich schläget,
Und das betrübte Marterheer.

NR. 12a (16) REZITATIV
EVANGELIST
*Und Hannas sandte ihn gebunden zu
dem Hohenpriester Kaiphas. Simon
Petrus stund und wärmete sich, da
sprachen sie zu ihm:*

NO. 11 (15) CHORALE
Who has struck you so,
my Salvation, and you with
    torments
handled so roughly?[20]
Indeed, you are not a sinner,
like we and our children;
you know nothing of misdeeds.

I, I and my sins,
which are as [numerous as] the
    grains
of sand on the seashore,
they have caused you
the sorrow that strikes you
and the grievous host of pain.[21]

NO. 12a (16) RECITATIVE
EVANGELIST
*And Annas sent him, bound, to the
high priest Caiaphas. Simon Peter
stood and warmed himself, when they
exclaimed to him:*

20. Placing chorales in close textual association with the biblical narrative is not to be understood as spontaneous expression of compassion [*Mitleid*] for Jesus but as exegesis of the sort found traditionally in Lutheran Baroque passion sermons, as becomes clear from the next stanza here. That is to say, Bach's commentary speaks not of the listener's fictive participation in the actual narrative but rather of a religious contemporaneity with it (Axmacher, "*Aus Liebe will mein Heiland Sterben*," 198). The approach is completely different in the *Brockes-Passion*, where, e.g., the allegorical characters the Daughter of Zion and the Faithful Soul continually ask Jesus whether he will remain silent, tell Pilate to be careful as he judges Jesus, ask the "murderers" if they know what they are doing, and the like.

21. This response, reproaching contemporary Christians for Jesus' Passion, is quite different from the responses provided by some of Bach's fellow composers and poets for this point and elsewhere in the narrative. In the *Brockes-Passion* settings, for example, the reaction to Jesus' being struck calls forth more of the ferocious language used against Jews in Brockes's poetry: branding them "wild animals," "foam of the world," and so on, even if elsewhere it blames Christians as well for the crucifixion. (What is noteworthy is that only Jews [see pp. 28–29 in the preceding essay] are described as subhuman: "these murderers . . . who are tigers, not humans," at no. 68 in Handel's setting, no. 72 in Telemann's; similar language — "Oh! my lamb [i.e., Jesus] in tiger claws [i.e., the Jewish leaders: "the chief priests and elders of the people"]" — appears in Bach only in the *St. Matthew Passion*, at the alto aria with accompanying chorus on Song of Solomon 6:1, "*Ach! nun ist mein Jesus hin!*"; my thanks to Bernard Greenberg for pointing this out.) Compare also Telemann's *St. John Passion* of 1745, whose commentary following Jesus' being struck reads: "Will you not wither, you sacrilegious hand, when you strike the great God of heavenly hosts . . . O forbearance!" (this is set with ferocious *stile concitato* repeated notes in the strings).

NR. 12b (17) CHOR
Bist du nicht seiner Jünger einer?

NO. 12b (17) CHORUS
Are you not one of his disciples?

NR. 12c (18) REZITATIV
EVANGELIST
Er leugnete aber und sprach:

NO. 12c (18) RECITATIVE
EVANGELIST
He denied it again and exclaimed:

PETRUS
Ich bin's nicht.

PETER
I am not.

EVANGELIST
Spricht des Hohenpriesters Knecht' einer, ein Gefreundter des, dem Petrus das Ohr abgehauen hatte:

EVANGELIST
One of the high priest's servants, a kinsman of him whose ear Peter had cut off, exclaims:

DIENER
Sahe ich dich nicht im Garten bei ihm?

ATTENDANT
Did I not behold you in the garden with him?

EVANGELIST
Da verleugnete Petrus abermal, und alsobald krähete der Hahn. Da gedachte Petrus an die Worte Jesu und ging hinaus und weinete bitterlich.

EVANGELIST
Then Peter denied it once more, and immediately the cock crowed. Then Peter remembered the words of Jesus[22] and went out and wept bitterly.

22. This sentence has been interpolated from Matthew 26:75. Peter is here remembering the words of Jesus in John 13:38 (Matthew 26:34).

NR. 13 (19) ARIE (TENOR)	NO. 13 (19) ARIA (TENOR)
Ach, mein Sinn,	O, my disposition,
Wo willt du endlich hin,	where do you at last intend to go;
Wo soll ich mich erquicken?	where shall I restore myself?
Bleib ich hier,	Shall I stay here,
Oder wünsch ich mir	or do I wish
Berg und Hügel auf den Rücken?	mountains and hills [to fall] upon my back?[23]
Bei der Welt ist gar kein Rat,	In the world there is no counsel whatsoever,
Und im Herzen	and in my heart
Stehn die Schmerzen	remain the agonies
Meiner Missetat,	of my misdeed:
Weil der Knecht den Herrn verleugnet hat.	for the servant has disavowed the Lord.[24]

NR. 14 (20) CHORAL	NO. 14 (20) CHORALE
Petrus, der nicht denkt zurück,	**Peter, who does not think back,**
Seinen Gott verneinet,	**denies his God;**
Der doch auf ein' ernsten Blick	**he, however, at a penetrating glance,[25]**
Bitterlichen weinet.	**weeps bitterly.**
Jesu, blicke mich auch an,	**Jesus, glance on me as well,**
Wenn ich nicht will büßen;	**whenever I am unrepentant;**
Wenn ich Böses hab getan,	**whenever I have done something evil,**
Rühre mein Gewissen!	**stir my conscience!**

23. This line alludes to Luke 23:26–31, where Jesus is depicted as saying to "the Daughters of Jerusalem," who are among the "great number of the people" lamenting his crucifixion: "the days are surely coming when they [the children of the Daughters of Jerusalem] shall say . . . to the mountains, 'Fall on us'; and to the hills, 'Cover us.'" I am indebted to Renate Steiger for explaining this continually mistranslated line to me.

24. This number is discussed on p. 17.

25. This refers to the *Heyland-Blick* ("gaze of the Savior") from Lutheran sermons on the passion narrative. As explained, e.g., in Heinrich Müller's (1631–75) passion sermons, several of which Bach owned, it is the warmth of Jesus' metaphoric gaze that melts the ice of Peter's heart into tears of repentance (Axmacher, *"Aus Liebe will mein Heiland Sterben,"* 36; Luke 22:61). This also helps to make sense of the references to Peter's continually trying to warm himself, each of them set here to similarly elaborate melodic formulas.

Parte secunda / Nach der Predigt

Part Two / *After the Sermon*

NR. 15 (21) CHORAL
Christus, der uns selig macht,
Kein Bös' hat begangen,
Der ward für uns in der Nacht
Als ein Dieb gefangen,
Geführt für gottlose Leut
Und fälschlich verklaget,
Verlacht, verhöhnt und verspeit,
Wie denn die Schrift saget.

NO. 15 (21) CHORALE
Christ, who makes us blessed,
[who] has committed no evil,
he was for us in the night
seized like a thief,
led before[26] godless[27] people
and falsely accused,
mocked, scorned, and spat upon,
as then the Scripture says.

NR. 16a (22) REZITATIV
EVANGELIST
*Da führeten sie Jesum von Kaiphas vor
das Richthaus, und es war frühe. Und
sie gingen nicht in das Richthaus, auf
daß sie nicht unrein würden, sondern
Ostern essen möchten. Da ging Pilatus
zu ihnen heraus und sprach:*

NO. 16a (22) RECITATIVE
EVANGELIST
*Then they led Jesus from Caiaphas
before the hall of judgment, and it was
early. And they did not go in the hall of
judgment, lest they would be defiled,[28]
but that they might eat [the] Passover
[meal]. Then Pilate went out to them
and exclaimed:*

PILATUS
*Was bringet ihr für Klage wider diesen
Menschen?*

PILATE
*What charge do you bring against this
man?*

EVANGELIST
Sie antworteten und sprachen zu ihm:

EVANGELIST
They answered and exclaimed to him:

26. See n. 17 above in the present translation.

27. *Gottlose Leut* refers to the Romans (the soldiers and Pilate, the Roman prefect of Judaea) in the hall of judgment to which Jesus is now being led. See no. 16a that follows. The stanzas of this well-known chorale move in sequence through the events of the passion narrative, and the stanza immediately following this one likewise concerns Jesus before Pilate. Bach's E-major harmonization of the last note in this Phrygian-mode chorale melody (whose pitches form the scale E–F–G–A–B–C–D–E, with E as the central one) and his particular string of closing bass notes work together to make this number sound as if it is pointing forward to the next one, no. 16a. They turn the libretto's period in *"wie denn die Schrift saget."* into a colon (*"wie denn die Schrift saget:"*).

28. There are laws from the Hebrew Scriptures that can be cited for this (Olearius: Numbers 9–11 [*Biblische Erklärung*, V, 779]), but the text may simply be projecting theological irony against "the Jews." Brown, *Death of the Messiah*, 744–46, cites from outside the Hebrew Scriptures also Mishnah *Oholot* 17.5, concerning defilement from rooms (like the hall of judgement) built over a burial place. With Pilate's continually coming in and going out and with some rearrangement of the story as compared to the other gospels, however, the Roman trial in John is structured as a chiasmus (Brown, *Death of the Messiah*, 758).

NR. 16b (23) CHOR
Wäre dieser nicht ein Übeltäter, wir
hätten dir ihn nicht überantwortet.

NO. 16b (23) CHORUS
Were this one not an evildoer, we
would not have given him over to you.

NR. 16c (24) REZITATIV
EVANGELIST
Da sprach Pilatus zu ihnen:

NO. 16c (24) RECITATIVE
EVANGELIST
Then Pilate exclaimed to them:

PILATUS
So nehmet ihr ihn hin und richtet ihn
nach eurem Gesetze!

PILATE
So take him away and judge him
according to your own law!

EVANGELIST
Da sprachen die Jüden zu ihm:

EVANGELIST
Then the Jews exclaimed to him:

NR. 16d (25) CHOR
Wir dürfen niemand töten.

NO. 16d (25) CHORUS
We are not permitted to put anyone to
death.[29]

NR. 16e (26) REZITATIV
EVANGELIST
Auf daß erfüllet würde das Wort Jesu,
welches er sagte, da er deutete, welches
Todes er sterben würde. Da ging Pilatus
wieder hinein in das Richthaus und rief
Jesu und sprach zu ihm:

NO. 16e (26) RECITATIVE
EVANGELIST
So that the word of Jesus would be
fulfilled, which he said when he
indicated what kind of death he would
die.[30] *Pilate then went back into the*
hall of judgment and summoned Jesus
and exclaimed to him:

PILATUS
Bist du der Jüden König?

PILATE
Are you the King of the Jews?

---

29. At least as Christian scriptural tradition had it, this was the case under the legal conditions of Roman rule. Current biblical scholarship supports the prohibition's historicity for the specific charges against Jesus depicted in the gospel, namely, being an evil-doer, making himself out to be divine, and making himself King of the Jews. There were other charges, however, for which Jews evidently were permitted to carry out death sentences, but not by crucifixion (see Brown, *Death of the Messiah,* 363–72, 748): for violating prohibitions against circulating in certain quarters of the Temple (Josephus, *War* 6.2.4; #124–26), and possibly for adultery (Mishnah *Sanhedrin* 7.2; cf. Leviticus 21:9 and Josephus, *Antiquities* 4.8.23; #248). The larger question, though, is whether and on what grounds Jews who opposed him could have wished Jesus dead. Sloyan, *Crucifixion of Jesus,* 50–51, contends that the most plausible reason involves Jesus' project under God as the restorer of Israel in a new and final age, a project that had no place in it for Judaism centered on the existing Temple in Jerusalem (i.e., explicitly or implicitly, Jesus publicly predicts or threatens the destruction of the Temple in all four canonical gospels; for extensive discussion, see Sanders, *Jesus and Judaism,* 61–76, passim).

30. John 12:32–33 (i.e., by crucifixion, the Roman method of execution).

EVANGELIST
Jesus antwortete:

JESUS
Redest du das von dir selbst, oder
haben's dir andere von mir gesagt?

EVANGELIST
Pilatus antwortete:

PILATUS
Bin ich ein Jüde? Dein Volk und die
Hohenpriester haben dich mir
überantwortet; was hast du getan?

EVANGELIST
Jesus antwortete:

JESUS
Mein Reich ist nicht von dieser Welt;
wäre mein Reich von dieser Welt, meine
Diener würden darob kämpfen, daß ich
den Jüden nicht überantwortet würde;
aber nun ist mein Reich nicht von
dannen.

EVANGELIST
Jesus answered:

JESUS
Do you speak of that on your own
[initiative], or have others said it to
you about me?

EVANGELIST
Pilate answered:

PILATE
Am I a Jew? Your people[31] *and the*
chief priests have given you over to me;
what have you done?

EVANGELIST
Jesus answered:

JESUS
My kingdom is not of this world; were
my kingdom of this world, my
attendants would fight on that account,
so that I would not be given over to the
Jews;[32] *again, as it is, my kingdom is*
not from here.

31. Neither Luther (*Das 18. und 19. Kapitel,* 308–9), Calov (*Die heilige Bibel,* V, 926), nor Olearius (*Biblische Erklärung,* V, 780–81) comments on Pilate's general indictment.

32. Many modern biblical scholars suggest that the gospel has Jesus speaking the language of Johannine Christian Jews (several generations after Jesus), not the language of Jesus' immediate situation (Brown, *Death of the Messiah,* 750; 759, n. 58). For example, while the gospel (9:22, 12:42, 16:2) says that some of Jesus' first followers feared expulsion, modern scholarship argues that these biblical characters actually represent later, Johannine Christian Jews. Some scholars (most prominently, Martyn, *History and Theology*) link the three gospel passages with an old Jewish prayer called the *Birkat Ha-Minim.* The exact wording (if there indeed was one) and meaning back in John's day of this "blessing [in this instance, a euphemism for "curse"] of the heretics [or, "sectarians"]" cannot be fully reconstructed, but there are no indications that its first-century version was directed at gentiles or that John's gospel knows anything of it. (For detailed criticism of Martyn's identification, see Kimelman, *"Birkat Ha-Minim* and the Lack of Evidence"; for further discussion, Horbury, "Benediction of the *Minim.*") Most scholars agree with Kimelman and would not see John as reflecting the *Birkat Ha-Minim:* it is important to note that the *Birkat* does not say anything about expulsion from the synagogue, and also that, quite apart from whether John is historically reliable in its reporting on fears of expulsion, the gospel nowhere says Jesus' followers were being cursed in the synagogue, which is the real point at issue with the *Birkat.* For a convenient, accessible survey, see Van der Horst, "Birkat ha-minim in Recent Research." (I am grateful to A.-J. Levine and Adele Reinhartz for helping me on this issue.) In Bach's time, John's expressions would have been believed to stem from Jesus' day (see Bach's church cantata *Am*

NR. 17 (27) CHORAL
Ach großer König, groß zu allen
Zeiten,
Wie kann ich gnugsam diese Treu
ausbreiten?
Keins Menschen Herze mag indes
ausdenken,
Was dir zu schenken.

Ich kann's mit meinen Sinnen nicht
erreichen,
Womit doch dein Erbarmen zu
vergleichen.
Wie kann ich dir denn deine
Liebestaten
Im Werk erstatten?

NR. 18a (28) REZITATIV
EVANGELIST
Da sprach Pilatus zu ihm:

PILATUS
So bist du dennoch ein König?

EVANGELIST
Jesus antwortete:

JESUS
*Du sagst's, ich bin ein König. Ich bin
dazu geboren und in die Welt kommen,
daß ich die Wahrheit zeugen soll. Wer
aus der Wahrheit ist, der höret meine
Stimme.*

EVANGELIST
Spricht Pilatus zu ihm:

PILATUS
Was ist Wahrheit?

NO. 17 (27) CHORALE
O great king, great through all the
ages,
how can I satisfactorily display this
faithfulness?
No human's heart could meanwhile
conceive of
something [fit] to give you.

I cannot with my capacities reach
anything
with which surely to compare your
mercy.
How can I, then, to you your acts of
love
with my deeds repay?

NO. 18a (28) RECITATIVE
EVANGELIST
Then Pilate exclaimed to him:

PILATE
So you are a king, then?

EVANGELIST
Jesus answered:

JESUS
*You say that I am a king.[33] For this I
am begotten and come into the world:
that I shall bear witness to the truth.
Whoever is of the truth, he hears my
voice.*

EVANGELIST
Pilate exclaims to him:

PILATE
What is truth?[34]

Abend aber desselbigen Sabbats [BWV 42], which makes negative comments about Jews of
Jesus' day; Olearius, *Biblische Erklärung,* V, 795). See also the discussion of the gospel's
expression "for fear of the Jews" here at pp. 21–23.

33. This number is discussed on p. 14.

34. Olearius, *Biblische Erklärung,* V, 781: "this was a derisive, ironic question" (also Calov,
Die heilige Bibel, V, 928).

EVANGELIST
Und da er das gesaget, ging er wieder hinaus zu den Jüden und spricht zu ihnen:

PILATUS
Ich finde keine Schuld an ihm. Ihr habt aber eine Gewohnheit, daß ich euch einen losgebe; wollt ihr nun, daß ich euch der Jüden König losgebe?

EVANGELIST
Da schrieen sie wieder allesamt und sprachen:

NR. 18b (29) CHOR
Nicht diesen, sondern Barrabam!

NR. 18c (30) REZITATIV
EVANGELIST
Barrabas aber war ein Mörder. Da nahm Pilatus Jesum und geißelte ihn.

NR. 19 (31) ARIOSO (BASS)
Betrachte, meine Seel, mit
    ängstlichem Vergnügen,
Mit bittrer Lust und halb
    beklemmtem Herzen
Dein höchstes Gut in Jesu Schmerzen,
Wie dir aus Dornen, so ihn stechen,

Die Himmelsschlüsselblumen blühn!
Du kannst viel süße Frucht von seiner
    Wermut brechen,

Drum sieh ohn Unterlaß auf ihn!

EVANGELIST
And when he [had] said this, he went back out to the Jews and exclaims to them:

PILATE
I find no guilt in him. But you have a custom[35] that I release one to you. Now do you want me to release to you the King of the Jews?

EVANGELIST
Then they shouted out in return, all together, and exclaimed:

NO. 18b (29) CHORUS
Not this one, but Barabbas![36]

NO. 18c (30) RECITATIVE
EVANGELIST
But Barabbas was a murderer. Pilate then took Jesus and scourged him.[37]

NO. 19 (31) ARIOSO (BASS)
Ponder, my soul, with anxious
    pleasure,
with bitter delight and half-uneasy
    heart,
in Jesus' agony your highest good;
how, for you, out of the thorns that
    pierce him,
the key-of-heaven flowers blossom!
You can break off much sweet fruit
    from his [bitter sorrow/]
    wormwood,[38]
so behold him without ceasing![39]

---

35. That is, according to this gospel, at Passover time. John 18:39 reads in the Luther Bibles: *daß ich euch einen auf Ostern* [at Passover] *losgebe* (i.e., the words *auf Ostern* are missing in the *St. John Passion*). Brown, *Death of the Messiah*, 814–20, indicates that there were instances of pardons but that there is no convincing extrabiblical evidence for a custom in Judaea of releasing a prisoner at Passover or at other feasts.

36. *Barabbas,* a name unknown in Jewish usage, means "son of the father"; Sloyan, *Crucifixion of Jesus*, 30.

37. Concerning this verse, see p. 28.

38. *Wermut* should be understood as a word play: its literal meaning is "wormwood," and its figurative meaning is "sorrow."

39. Concerning the poetic source for this number, see p. 28.

NR. 20 (32) ARIE (TENOR)
Erwäge, wie sein blutgefärbter Rücken

In allen Stücken
Den Himmel gleiche geht,
   Daran, nachdem die
     Wasserwogen
   Von unsrer Sündflut sich
     verzogen,
   Der allerschönste Regenbogen
   Als Gottes Gnadenzeichen steht!

NR. 21a (33) REZITATIV
EVANGELIST
*Und die Kriegsknechte flochten eine
Krone von Dornen und satzten sie auf
sein Haupt und legten ihm ein
Purpurkleid an und sprachen:*

NR. 21b (34) CHOR
Sei gegrüßet, lieber Jüdenkönig!

NR. 21c (35) REZITATIV
EVANGELIST
*Und gaben ihm Backenstreiche. Da ging
Pilatus wieder heraus und sprach zu
ihnen:*

PILATUS
*Sehet, ich führe ihn heraus zu euch, daß
ihr erkennet, daß ich keine Schuld an
ihm finde.*

EVANGELIST
*Also ging Jesus heraus und trug eine
Dornenkrone und Purpurkleid. Und er
sprach zu ihnen:*

PILATUS
Sehet, welch ein Mensch!

NO. 20 (32) ARIE (TENOR)
Consider, how his blood-tinged
   back,
in all aspects
is just like the sky.
     Thereon, after the floodwaves

   of our sins' deluge have passed
     by,
   the most beautiful rainbow
   remains as a sign of God's grace!

NO. 21a (33) RECITATIVE
EVANGELIST
*And the soldiers plaited a crown of
thorns and placed it upon his head and
put on him a purple robe and
exclaimed:*

NO. 21b (34) CHORUS
Greetings, dear King of the Jews![40]

NO. 21c (35) RECITATIVE
EVANGELIST
*And gave him blows to the face. Then
Pilate went back out and exclaimed to
them:*[41]

PILATE
*Behold, I am leading him out to you, so
that you will recognize that I find no
guilt in him.*

EVANGELIST
*Thus Jesus went out, wearing a crown
of thorns and purple robe. And he
[Pilate] exclaimed to them:*

PILATE
Behold, what a man!

---

40. This number is discussed on pp. 15–16.

41. The location (outside the hall of judgment) makes it clear that this "them" refers to the Jews (see no. 16a), not to the Roman soldiers (who are inside the hall of judgment).

EVANGELIST
Da ihn die Hohenpriester und die
Diener sahen, schrieen sie und sprachen:

EVANGELIST
When the chief priests and the
attendants beheld him, they shouted
out and exclaimed:

NR. 21d (36) CHOR
Kreuzige, kreuzige!

NO. 21d (36) CHORUS
Crucify, crucify![42]

NR. 21e (37) REZITATIV
EVANGELIST
Pilatus sprach zu ihnen:

NO. 21e (37) RECITATIVE
EVANGELIST
Pilate exclaimed to them:

PILATUS
Nehmet ihr ihn hin und kreuziget ihn;
denn ich finde keine Schuld an ihm!

PILATE
Take him away and crucify him;[43] *for*
I find no guilt in him!

EVANGELIST
Die Jüden antworteten ihm:

EVANGELIST
The Jews answered him:

NR. 21f (38) CHOR
Wir haben ein Gesetz, und nach dem
Gesetz soll er sterben; denn er hat sich
selbst zu Gottes Sohn gemacht.

NO. 21f (38) CHORUS
We have a law, and according to the[44]
law he ought to die:[45] *for he has made*
himself the Son of God.

---

42. The long-note dissonances echo the woodwind parts from the opening chorus (Terry, *Bach: The Passions*, 23). Because voices cross each other, such gestures are called "cross motives" by writers on music. Schleuning, ". . . auf daß zur heil'gen Liebe," 137–38, sees in the parallel movement no. 23d (misidentified as no. 21d) an expression of antisemitism similar to Richard Wagner's.

43. This reflects mockery on Pilate's part (Olearius: "that was [Pilate's] scoffing. Cf. John 18:31" [*Biblische Erklärung*, V, 785]), as he should know that the chief priests and attendants are not permitted to put Jesus to death on the charges brought against him. They evidently understand Pilate not to be serious, for they continue pressing him for Jesus' death.

44. The melody strikingly jumps to a higher note on the offbeat for the word *dem*, making it sound like the chorus is saying "and according to *this* law"; also the musical accent on *Wir* is probably deliberate: "*We* have a law" (Dürr, *Johannes-Passion*, 85).

45. Calov, *Die heilige Bibel*, V, 934: "Leviticus 24:16 . . . as a blasphemer against God"; Olearius (*Biblische Erklärung*, V, 778, 780): Deuteronomy 13:5; Olearius (*Biblische Erklärung*, V, 785): Leviticus 24:16, adding "they believed [*vermeynten*] this would be against the majesty of the One God — Deuteronomy 6:4." The notion of blasphemy comes from the translation used by Greek-speaking Jews and Christians, the Septuagint (see n. 8 above in the present translation).

NR. 21g (39) REZITATIV
EVANGELIST
*Da Pilatus das Wort hörete, fürchtet' er
sich noch mehr und ging wieder hinein
in das Richthaus und spricht zu Jesu:*

PILATUS
Von wannen bist du?

EVANGELIST
*Aber Jesus gab ihm keine Antwort. Da
sprach Pilatus zu ihm:*

PILATUS
*Redest du nicht mit mir? Weißest du
nicht, daß ich Macht habe, dich zu
kreuzigen, und Macht habe, dich
loszugeben?*

EVANGELIST
Jesus antwortete:

JESUS
*Du hättest keine Macht über mich,
wenn sie dir nicht wäre von oben herab
gegeben; darum, der mich dir
überantwortet hat, der hat's größ're
Sünde.*

NO. 21g (39) RECITATIVE
EVANGELIST
*When Pilate heard those words, he was
yet more afraid[46] and went back into
the hall of judgment and exclaims to
Jesus:*

PILATE
Where do you come from?

EVANGELIST
*But Jesus gave him no answer. Then
Pilate exclaimed to him:*

PILATE
*Will you not speak with me? Don't you
know that I have power to crucify you,
and have power to release you?*

EVANGELIST
Jesus answered:

JESUS
*You would have no power over me, if it
were not handed down to you from on
high;[47] therefore, [the one] who has
given me over to you, he has the greater
sin.[48]*

---

46. Luther, like many modern biblical interpreters, believed Pilate was afraid not that Jesus might be the Son of the one God proclaimed by Jews but that he was a potentially troublesome son of the pagan gods (Olearius, *Biblische Erklärung*, V, 785; Luther, *Das 18. und 19. Kapitel*, 352, which is quoted in Calov, *Die heilige Bibel*, V, 935).

47. Jesus again sings the melodic formula for Pilate's law statements (i.e., on the syllables *wenn sie dir nicht wä-re von o-ben her-ab ge-ge-ben*), likewise with A as the home pitch (see pp. 14–15). There is a rapid shift away from it, however, by substituting C with C-sharp (Ex. 23: Kuijken, CD 2, track 7, 0:44–1:02), so that the centrally important number that follows, "*Durch dein Gefängnis*," can appear in the key of E, which has four sharps. Significantly, the German word for "sharp" (the sign #) is *Kreuz* (cross).

48. That is, Pilate is to be considered sinful as well. "[Jesus] does not excuse Pilate but rather shows him that he is guilty" (Calov, *Die heilige Bibel*, V, 937, quoting Luther). The greater sin presumably lies either with Caiaphas, who, technically, has turned him over to Pilate, or with Jesus' disciple Judas. Luther suggests that the singular *der* may here as elsewhere in the Bible also be taken as a plural: "[This *der* is] Caiaphas, Annas, Judas, and all those in this gang who have taken Christ into custody and given him over to Pilate" (Calov, *Die heilige Bibel*, V, 937). On the notion of a hierarchy of guilt (Romans - Jews - Protestant Christians), see p. 35.

EVANGELIST
Von dem an trachtete Pilatus, wie er ihn losließe.

EVANGELIST
From this, henceforth, Pilate sought how he might release him.

NR. 22 (40) CHORAL
Durch dein Gefängnis, Gottes Sohn,

Ist uns die Freiheit kommen;
Dein Kerker ist der Gnadenthron,
Die Freistatt aller Frommen;
Denn gingst du nicht die
    Knechtschaft ein,
Müßt unsre Knechtschaft ewig sein.

NO. 22 (40) CHORALE
Through your imprisonment, Son of God,

freedom has[49] come to us;
your dungeon is the throne of grace,
the refuge of all the devout;
for had you not entered into
    servitude,
our servitude would have had to be
    everlasting.

NR. 23a (41) REZITATIV
EVANGELIST
Die Jüden aber schrieen und sprachen:

NO. 23a (41) RECITATIVE
EVANGELIST
But the Jews shouted out and exclaimed:

NR. 23b (42) CHOR
Lässest du diesen los, so bist du des Kaisers Freund nicht; denn wer sich zum Könige machet, der ist wider den Kaiser.

NO. 23b (42) CHORUS
If you release this[50] one, then you are no friend of the emperor's; for whoever makes himself a king is against the emperor.[51]

NR. 23c (43) REZITATIV
EVANGELIST
Da Pilatus das Wort hörete, führete er Jesum heraus, und satzte sich auf den Richtstuhl, an der Stätte, die da heißet: Hochpflaster, auf Ebräisch aber: Gabbatha. Es war aber der Rüsttag in Ostern um die sechste Stunde, und er spricht zu den Jüden:

NO. 23c (43) RECITATIVE
EVANGELIST
When Pilate heard those words, he led Jesus out and sat himself on the judgment seat,[52] at the place that is called "High Pavement," but "Gabbatha" in Hebrew.[53] It was, however, the preparation day in Passover, at the sixth hour, and he [Pilate] exclaims to the Jews:

---

49. The original words to this number, evidently not a chorale but an aria, believed written by Christian Heinrich Postel (1658–1705), here reads *Muß uns die Freiheit kommen* ("freedom *must* come to us"). The *St. John Passion* tranforms the meaning by changing the line to "*has* come to us" (Smend, *Bach in Köthen*, 145).

50. The musical accent on the first syllable of *diesen* is presumably deliberate: "If you let *this* one go" (Dürr, *Johannes-Passion*, 85).

51. Concerning the significance of the repetition of earlier music at this point and elsewhere, see pp. 30–33.

52. Some Bibles understand John's Greek to mean "and sat *him* [Jesus] on the judgment seat," picturing Jesus mocked by Pilate as a judge or king (Brown, *Death of the Messiah*, 844). Luther, however, reads the Greek to mean that Pilate is on the judgment seat (Luther Bibles

PILATUS
Sehet, das ist euer König!

PILATE
Behold, this is your king!

EVANGELIST
Sie schrieen aber:

EVANGELIST
But they shouted out:

NR. 23d (44) CHOR
Weg, weg mit dem, kreuzige ihn!

NO. 23d (44) CHORUS
Away, away with him, crucify him!

NR. 23e (45) REZITATIV
EVANGELIST
Spricht Pilatus zu ihnen:

NO. 23e (45) RECITATIVE
EVANGELIST
Pilate exclaims to them:

PILATUS
Soll ich euren König kreuzigen?

PILATE
Shall I crucify your king?

EVANGELIST
Die Hohenpriester antworteten:

EVANGELIST
The chief priests answered:

NR. 23f (46) CHOR
Wir haben keinen König denn den Kaiser.

NO. 23f (46) CHORUS
We have no king but the emperor.[54]

---

employ the reflexive *Pilatus . . . satzte sich,* "Pilate sat himself"), and Luther stresses that Pilate went there to make sure his judgment was completely open and in public (Luther, *Das 18. und 19. Kapitel,* 372–73; quoted in Calov, *Die heilige Bibel,* V, 938). With Pilate on the judgment seat, the scene reflects a formal judgment on his part, which is not to say that he proceeded according to the requirements of Roman law for citizens — Jesus was, after all, not a Roman citizen (Brown, *Death of the Messiah,* 715). Thus in Lutheran interpretation it is not only the Jewish religious authorities who make a decision about Jesus (see John 11:47–53).

53. The "Hebrew" word *Gabbatha* is actually Aramaic (Brown, *Death of the Messiah,* 709).

54. Listeners are presumably to understand the chief priests to be saying "we have no Jewish king right now." Jews had not been led to expect a messiah who acted like Jesus of Nazareth (Neusner, *A Rabbi,* passim; Brown, *Introduction to New Testament Christology,* 160–61, n. 220; Sloyan, *Crucifixion of Jesus,* 54–55); in Jesus' day, Jews had no human king of their own, and it would have been part and parcel of a chief priest's framework of belief to hold that his only divine king was the one Almighty God, not a human/divine person associated or equated with God. Olearius, *Biblische Erklärung,* V, 786, reads for the commentary on this passage: "*Caesar;* [cf.] vs. 12; *NB* John 18:31; the [Jewish] government was defunct [*verlohren*]; more information on that, Zechariah 11:6."

NR. 23g (47) REZITATIV
EVANGELIST

*Da überantwortete er ihn, daß er
gekreuziget würde. Sie nahmen aber
Jesum und führeten ihn hin. Und er
trug sein Kreuz und ging hinaus zur
Stätte, die da heißet Schädelstätt, welche
heißet auf Ebräisch: Golgatha.*

NO. 23g (47) RECITATIVE
EVANGELIST

*Then he gave him over, that he would
be crucified. They took Jesus again and
led him away. And he carried his cross
and went out to the place that is called
"Place of Skulls," which is called in
Hebrew, "Golgatha."* [55]

NR. 24 (48) ARIE (BASS) MIT
CHOR

Eilt, ihr angefochtnen Seelen,
Geht aus euren Marterhöhlen,
Eilt — Wohin? — nach Golgatha!
    Nehmet an des Glaubens Flügel,
    Flieht — Wohin? — zum
      Kreuzeshügel,
    Eure Wohlfahrt blüht allda!

NO. 24 (48) ARIA (BASS) WITH
CHORUS

Hurry, you besieged souls,
leave your dens of torment,[56]
hurry — where? — to Golgotha!
    Embrace faith's wings;[57]
    flee — where? — to the cross's
      hilltop;
    your welfare blossoms there!

NR. 25a (49) REZITATIV
EVANGELIST

*Allda kreuzigten sie ihn, und mit ihm
zween andere zu beiden Seiten, Jesum
aber mitten inne. Pilatus aber schrieb
eine Überschrift und satzte sie auf das
Kreuz, und war geschrieben: "Jesus von
Nazareth, der Jüden König." Diese
Überschrift lasen viel Jüden, denn die
Stätte war nahe bei der Stadt, da Jesus
gekreuziget ist. Und es war geschrieben
auf ebräische, griechische und lateinische
Sprache. Da sprachen die Hohenpriester
der Jüden zu Pilato:*

NO. 25a (49) RECITATIVE
EVANGELIST

*There they[58] crucified him, and with
him two others, one on either side, but
Jesus in the middle. But Pilate wrote a
title and put it on the cross, and [it]
was written, "Jesus of Nazareth, the
King of the Jews."[59] Many Jews read
this title, for the place where Jesus was
crucified was near the city. And it was
written in the Hebrew, Greek, and
Latin languages. Then the chief priests
of the Jews exclaimed to Pilate:*

---

55. *Golgotha* is actually closer to the Aramaic than the Hebrew equivalent (Brown, *Death of the Messiah*, 936).

56. Concerning this number, see pp. 29–30.

57. This image should presumably be understood in light of Luther's famous notion of the Christian's being at the same time both righteous and sinful (*simul iustus et peccator*). According to Luther, Christians in this life are always sinners, but God does not reckon them as sinners on account of their undeserved gift of faith in Christ. The God of wrath does not "see" their sin, because it is covered by the protective "wings" of the Savior. For a concise introduction to this subject, see Westerholm, *Israel's Law and the Church's Faith*, 3–12. Jesus as a brood hen protecting his followers under his wings is a favorite image in Luther. See, e.g., the commentary on Matthew 23:37 in Calov, *Die heilige Bibel*, V, 235–36; and Luther's commentary on John 8:12, with cross-reference to Malachi 4:2, in Luther, *Sermons on the Gospel of John*, 324–25.

58. According to Luther, this "they" refers to the Roman soldiers. See *Das 18. und 19. Kapitel*, 390 (quoted in Calov, *Die heilige Bibel*, V, 943), where Luther notes that Pilate had

NR. 25b (50) CHOR
Schreibe nicht: der Jüden König,
sondern daß er gesaget habe: Ich bin der
Jüden König.

NO. 25b (50) CHORUS
Write not: "The King of the Jews";
rather, that "he said:[60] *'I am the King*
of the Jews.'"[61]

NR. 25c (51) REZITATIV
EVANGELIST
Pilatus antwortet:

NO. 25c (51) RECITATIVE
EVANGELIST
Pilate answers:

PILATUS
Was ich geschrieben habe, das habe ich
geschrieben.

PILATE
What I have written, I have written.

NR. 26 (52) CHORAL
In meines Herzens Grunde,
Dein Nam und Kreuz allein
Funkelt all Zeit und Stunde,
Drauf kann ich fröhlich sein.
Erschein mir in dem Bilde
Zu Trost in meiner Not,
Wie du, Herr Christ, so milde

Dich hast geblut' zu Tod!

NO. 26 (52) CHORALE
In the bottom of my heart,
your name and cross alone
shines forth every age and hour,
for which I can be joyful.
Appear before me in the image,
as comfort in my distress:
how you, Lord Christ, so
    abundantly[62]
did bleed to death!

---

not even commanded that Jesus should be crucified along with the two murderers but that the soldiers did this as a service to the malicious chief priests. See also the comment concerning the "they" in no. 27a (at n. 63 below in the present translation).

59. The title, specifying the charge on which, according to John's gospel, the Romans executed Jesus, is most likely historically accurate, according to Brown, *Death of the Messiah*, 968, who, citing Josephus, *Antiquities* 17.10.8, 10; #285, 295, reports that violent Roman reaction to claims of kingship are evident from crucifixions performed by Varus, the Roman governor of Syria. But the title's appearance in three languages is another matter (Brown, 965).

60. *Er gesaget habe* (rather than *gesagt hat* or *gesagt hätte*) is not perfect subjunctive but oblique expression (old form).

61. The chief priests may have wished the many Jews visiting Jersualem for Passover to see from the title that Jesus was dangerous to "the people" both politically (*König* — claiming power when in a province under Roman rule) and religiously (*Ich bin* — claiming divinity). Olearius links the title with the I AM material in John 18:37 and 18:5 (*Biblische Erklärung*, V, 781, 787).

62. The word *milde* here means not "calmly" but "abundantly," an understanding found also in Müller's passion sermons (see n. 25 above in the present translation); for the theological and etymological backgrounds, see Steiger, "Wo soll ich," 78–79. *Milde* is used in this same sense in the aria *"Können Tränen meiner Wangen"* from Bach's *St. Matthew Passion*.

NR. 27a (53) REZITATIV
EVANGELIST

Die Kriegsknechte aber, da sie Jesum
gekreuziget hatten, nahmen seine
Kleider und machten vier Teile, einem
jeglichen Kriegesknechte sein Teil, dazu
auch den Rock. Der Rock aber war
ungenähet, von oben an gewürket durch
und durch. Da sprachen sie
untereinander:

NR. 27b (54) CHOR

Lasset uns den nicht zerteilen, sondern
darum losen, wes er sein soll.

NR. 27c (55) REZITATIV
EVANGELIST

Auf daß erfüllet würde die Schrift, die
da saget: "Sie haben meine Kleider unter
sich geteilet und haben über meinen
Rock das Los geworfen." Solches taten
die Kriegsknechte. Es stund aber bei
dem Kreuze Jesu seine Mutter und
seiner Mutter Schwester, Maria,
Kleophas Weib, und Maria Magdalena.
Da nun Jesus seine Mutter sahe und den
Jünger dabei stehen, den er lieb hatte,
spricht er zu seiner Mutter:

NO. 27a (53) RECITATIVE
EVANGELIST

The soldiers, however, when they[63] *had*
crucified Jesus, took his clothes and
made four parts, to each soldier his
part;[64] *in addition [they took], indeed,*
the robe. But the robe was seamless,
woven in one piece from top to bottom.
Then they exclaimed among themselves:

NO. 27b (54) CHORUS

Let us not cut it up, but toss for it, [to
see] whose it shall be.

NO. 27c (55) RECITATIVE
EVANGELIST

So that the scripture would be fulfilled,
which says: "They have parted my
clothing among themselves and have
cast lots for my robe."[65] *Such a thing*
the soldiers did. But there stood by the
cross of Jesus his mother and his
mother's sister, Mary, Cleophas's
wife,[66] *and Mary Magdalene. Now*
when Jesus beheld his mother and the
disciple whom he loved standing
nearby, he exclaims to his mother:

63. This "they" (like the one in no. 25a) refers to the Roman soldiers, as is clear from Luther's commentary on this passage. Luther writes: "Here St. John makes a very assiduous text out of the Lord Christ's robe and clothes and says that the soldiers, thus having crucified Christ, divided his clothes . . ." (*Das 18. und 19. Kapitel*, 396; quoted in Calov, *Die heilige Bibel*, V, 945).

64. Squads of four Roman soldiers (Greek: *tetradion*) seem to have been common. See Brown, *Death of the Messiah*, 954, who also points to the squads of Acts 12:4.

65. Psalm 22:19 (Calov, *Die heilige Bibel*, V, 945; Olearius, *Biblische Erklärung*, V, 787).

66. Biblical interpretation has come up with a variety of conclusions on how many women John's Greek text refers to, how the text's Clopas is related to one of the women, and whether he and the Cleopas of Luke 24:18 are the same person; see Brown, *Death of the Messiah*, 1013–19. Luther's translation is not exactly transparent, either. Bach's music for this verse projects the sense that "[Jesus'] mother's sister," "Mary," and "Cleophas's wife" all refer to the same person. That way of reckoning — namely, that there are three women by the cross: Jesus' mother, her sister, and Mary Magdalene — conforms to the three women discussed in Luther's complicated commentary on this passage (*Das 18. und 19. Kapitel*, 401–3); it also conforms to Olearius's numbering and identification (*Biblische Erklärung*, V, 787). Neither Luther nor Olearius appears troubled by the fact that two sisters would be named Mary. (In the gospel of John the mother of Jesus is not identified by name.)

JESUS
Weib, siehe, das ist dein Sohn!

EVANGELIST
Darnach spricht er zu dem Jünger:

JESUS
Siehe, das ist deine Mutter!

NR. 28 (56) CHORAL
Er nahm alles wohl in acht
In der letzten Stunde,
Seine Mutter noch bedacht,
Setzt ihr ein' Vormunde.
O Mensch, mache Richtigkeit,

Gott und Menschen liebe,
Stirb darauf ohn alles Leid,
Und dich nicht betrübe!

NR. 29 (57) REZITATIV
EVANGELIST
*Und von Stund an nahm sie der Jünger
zu sich. Darnach, als Jesus wußte, daß
schon alles vollbracht war, daß die
Schrift erfüllet würde, spricht er:*

JESUS
Mich dürstet!

JESUS
Woman, behold, this is your son!

EVANGELIST
After that he exclaims to the disciple:

JESUS
Behold, this is your mother!

NO. 28 (56) CHORALE
He thought of everything
in the final hour;
his mother still [being] considered,
[he] assigns her a guardian.
O humankind, set everything in
order,[67]
love God and humankind,
die afterwards without any woe,
and be untroubled!

NO. 29 (57) RECITATIVE
EVANGELIST
*And from that hour forth the disciple
took her to his own. After this, since
Jesus knew that everything had already
been accomplished, so that the Scripture
would be fulfilled,[68] he exclaims:*

JESUS
I thirst![69]

67. For *mache Richtigkeit*, compare Isaiah's words to Hezekiah in Isaiah 38:1. This line may have more to do with "setting one's house in order" than "being good." My thanks to Renate Steiger for this observation.

68. Lutheran Baroque theologians refer to Psalm 22, Psalm 42, or Job 15:16 (Axmacher, *"Aus Liebe will mein Heiland Sterben,"* 47, 139); Olearius: Psalms 22, 42, 69, and 73 (*Biblische Erklärung*, V, 788).

69. Nearly every extant Lutheran Baroque passion sermon provides the explanation that Jesus spiritually thirsted "for our blessedness" (also Olearius, *Biblische Erklärung*, V, 788). This is part of Jesus' accepting the "cup" that his Father had given him (Axmacher, *"Aus Liebe will mein Heiland Sterben,"* 139).

EVANGELIST
Da stund ein Gefäße voll Essigs. Sie
fülleten aber einen Schwamm mit Essig
und legten ihn um einen Isopen, und
hielten es ihm dar zum Munde. Da nun
Jesus den Essig genommen hatte, sprach
er:

EVANGELIST
There stood a vessel filled with vinegar.
But they[70] filled a sponge with vinegar,
set it upon a hyssop[71] branch, and held
it up to his mouth. Now when Jesus
had taken the vinegar, he exclaimed:

JESUS
Es ist vollbracht!

JESUS
It is accomplished!

NR. 30 (58) ARIE (ALT)
Es ist vollbracht!
O Trost vor die gekränkten Seelen!
Die Trauernacht
Läßt nun die letzte Stunde zählen.
Der Held aus Juda siegt mit Macht

Und schließt den Kampf.
Es ist vollbracht!

NO. 30 (58) ARIA (ALTO)
It is accomplished!
O comfort for[72] the afflicted souls!
The night of mourning
now counts the final hour.
The hero from Judah triumphs with
    power
and closes the battle.
It is accomplished![73]

NR. 31 (59) REZITATIV
EVANGELIST
Und neiget das Haupt und verschied.

NO. 31 (59) RECITATIVE
EVANGELIST
And bowed his head and expired.

70. The textual antecedents for this "they" are Jesus' mother and his Beloved Disciple, but John 19:27 seems to put an end to the mother's involvement in the scene. Thus most commentators take this "they" to refer to the Roman soldiers, who are active in 19:23–24 and who would have had access to Jesus and the vinegar (Brown, *Death of the Messiah*, 1074–75).

71. The gospel's purpose here in mentioning hyssop is probably to echo the paschal lamb imagery of Exodus 12:22 (so Olearius, *Biblische Erklärung*, V, 788). Thus we could leave aside the banal question of whether hyssop would have been right at hand, or whether hyssop branches of the sort then found in Judaea could have physically supported a vinegar-filled sponge (see Brown, *Death of the Messiah*, 1076).

72. As is the case at several other spots in the libretto, the old form *vor* appears where today's German would use *für*.

73. This number is discussed on pp. 18–20.

NR. 32 (60) ARIE (BASS) UND
    CHORAL

Mein teurer Heiland, laß dich fragen,
    Jesu, der du warest tot,
Da du nunmehr ans Kreuz geschlagen

Und selbst gesaget: Es ist vollbracht,

    Lebest nun ohn Ende,

Bin ich vom Sterben frei gemacht?
    In der letzten Todesnot,
    Nirgend mich hinwende
Kann ich durch deine Pein und
    Sterben
Das Himmelreich ererben?
Ist aller Welt Erlösung da?
    Als zu dir, der mich versühnt,

    O du lieber Herre!
Du kannst vor Schmerzen zwar nichts
    sagen;
    Gib mir nur, was du verdient,

Doch neigest du das Haupt
Und sprichst stillschweigend: ja.
    Mehr ich nicht begehre!

NO. 32 (60) ARIA (BASS) AND
    CHORALE[74]

My precious Saviour, let me ask you:
    Jesus, you who were dead,
since you by this time [are] nailed to
    the cross
and [have] yourself said, "It is
    accomplished,"
    [but who] now live[s] without
    end,
have I been made free from death?
    in the final throes of death,
    [I] turn myself nowhere
Can I through your pain and death

inherit the kingdom of heaven?
Is redemption of all the world here?
    but to you, who made
    propitiation for me,
    O you dear Lord!
You can, in agony, it is true, say
    nothing;
    Give me only what you [have]
    merited;
but you bow your head
and exclaim in silence, "Yes."
    more I do not desire!

74. In this number, there are two commentary poems sung simultaneously, not one long poem.

NR. 33 (61) REZITATIV
EVANGELIST

Und siehe da, der Vorhang im Tempel zerriß in zwei Stück von oben an bis unten aus. Und die Erde erbebete, und die Felsen zerrissen, und die Gräber täten sich auf, und stunden auf viele Leiber der Heiligen.

NO. 33 (61) RECITATIVE
EVANGELIST

And behold then, the veil in the Temple rent in two pieces from top to bottom.[75] And the earth quaked,[76] and the rocks rent, and the graves opened, and there arose the bodies of many saints.[77]

NR. 34 (62) ARIOSO (TENOR)

Mein Herz, indem die ganze Welt
Bei Jesu Leiden gleichfalls leidet,
Die Sonne sich in Trauer kleidet,
Der Vorhang reißt, der Fels zerfällt,
Die Erde bebt, die Gräber spalten,

Weil sie den Schöpfer sehn erkalten,

Was willst du deines Ortes tun?

NO. 34 (62) ARIOSO (TENOR)

My heart, — while the entire world
with Jesus' suffering likewise suffers,
the sun clothes itself in mourning,
the veil tears, the rock crumbles,
the earth quakes, the graves split open,
because they behold the creator growing cold
— what do you for your part want to do?

NR. 35 (63) ARIE (SOPRAN)

Zerfließe, mein Herze, in Fluten der Zähren
Dem Höchsten zu Ehren!
  Erzähle der Welt und dem Himmel die Not:
  Dein Jesus ist tot!

NO. 35 (63) ARIA (SOPRANO)

Dissolve, my heart, in floods of tears[78]
to honor the Most High!
  Declare to the world and to heaven the distress:
  your Jesus is dead!

---

75. Calov, *Die heilige Bibel,* V, 292: "in order to indicate that Christ, the only high priest, by his own blood entered the Most Holy Place [*das Allerheiligste,* the Temple's "holy of holies"] by this time, and earned for us an everlasting redemption. Hebrews 9:12. That even by Christ's death the path to the Throne of Grace indeed opens up. Hebrews 4:16, 10:19–20."

76. There are in the Hebrew Scriptures many examples of the earth shaking as a sign of divine judgment of God's people or of the last times (Brown, *Death of the Messiah,* 1121–22, lists Judges 5:4; Isaiah 5:25, 24:18; Ezekiel 38:19; Joel 2:10; and others). Bach's Calov Bible Commentary at this point refers to Joel 2:10–11 (*Die heilige Bibel,* V, 292).

77. Lutheranism held that the true church of God had been established before the fall of Adam and Eve into sin and, further, that all messianic promises in the Hebrew Scriptures refer to Jesus of Nazareth. Thus, living by faith in God's promises, the saintly Israelites of the Hebrew Scriptures were considered to be part of the true church (Edwards, *Luther's Last Battles,* 123).

78. This is the initial reaction. The spiritually more mature response, recognizing the positive significance of the event, comes at no. 39: *ich nun weiter* nicht *beweine* ("I will no longer bewail").

NR. 36 (64) REZITATIV
EVANGELIST

Die Jüden aber, dieweil es der Rüsttag
war, daß nicht die Leichname am
Kreuze blieben den Sabbat über (denn
desselbigen Sabbats Tag war sehr groß),
baten sie Pilatum, daß ihre Beine
gebrochen und sie abgenommen würden.
Da kamen die Kriegsknechte und
brachen dem ersten die Beine und dem
andern, der mit ihm gekreuziget war.
Als sie aber zu Jesu kamen, da sie sahen,
daß er schon gestorben war, brachen sie
ihm die Beine nicht; sondern der
Kriegsknechte einer eröffnete seine Seite
mit einem Speer, und alsobald ging Blut
und Wasser heraus.

NO. 36 (64) RECITATIVE
EVANGELIST

But the Jews, because it was the
preparation day, that the corpses might
not remain on the cross during the
sabbath (for that particular sabbath
was a very great day[79]), asked Pilate
that their legs would be broken and
that they would be taken down. Then
the soldiers came and broke the legs of
the first and of the other who had been
crucified with him. But when they
came to Jesus, because they beheld that
he was already dead, they did not break
his legs; rather, one of the soldiers
opened[80] his side with a spear, and
immediately blood and water went out.

---

79. "Great day," because this was the sabbath in Passover (Olearius, *Biblische Erklärung*, V, 789). According to Deuteronomy 21:22–23, the law to this effect held true for any day (a reference to Deuteronomy 21 appears here in Calov, *Die heilige Bibel*, V, 948). Deuteronomy's "hanging on a tree," however, may refer to hanging *after* execution, and one might also question whether Deuteronomy's expression refers to crucifixions at all; compare Crossan, *Who Killed Jesus?*, 163, with Brown, *Death of the Messiah*, 731–32.

80. It is not clear how John's Greek ought to be translated here. Augustine and others read it as "opened" (Brown, *Death of the Messiah*, 1177). Luther too, following Augustine (Luther, *Hauspostille*, 818), translates it "opened." He points out that blood and water cannot flow from dead bodies and, seeing forgiveness of sin written all over the event, suggests this is a miracle that points to the sacraments of communion and baptism in the name of Jesus (Calov, *Die heilige Bibel*, V, 949–51; likewise Olearius, *Biblische Erklärung*, V, 792). Neither sacrament is expressly instituted in John's gospel (see Käsemann, *Testament of Jesus*, 32–33; cf. John 3:5 and 6:51–58). Baptismal imagery also appears in no. 20.

Und der das gesehen hat, der hat es	And he who has beheld this has borne
bezeuget, und sein Zeugnis ist wahr,	witness to it, and his witness is true,
und derselbige weiß, daß er die	and this same one knows that he says
Wahrheit saget, auf daß ihr gläubet.	the truth, so that you may believe. For
Denn solches ist geschehen, auf daß die	such a thing has happened so that the
Schrift erfüllet würde: "Ihr sollet ihm	scripture would be fulfilled: "You shall
kein Bein zerbrechen." Und abermal	break none of its bones."[81] And another
spricht eine andere Schrift: "Sie werden	scripture exclaims once more: "They
sehen, in welchen sie gestochen haben."	will behold whom they have pierced."[82]

NR. 37 (65) CHORAL	NO. 37 (65) CHORALE
O hilf, Christe, Gottes Sohn,	O help, Christ, Son of God,
Durch dein bitter Leiden,	through your bitter suffering,
Daß wir dir stets untertan	that we, ever to you submissive,
All Untugend meiden,	may shun all [spiritual and moral] failing,
Deinen Tod und sein Ursach	[and] your death and the reason for it[83]
Fruchtbarlich bedenken,	fruitfully consider
Dafür, wiewohl arm und schwach,	— for which, though poor and weak,
Dir Dankopfer schenken!	[we] give you a thanksoffering!

81. Exodus 12:46 in Calov (*Die heilige Bibel,* V, 953; cf. Olearius, *Biblische Erklärung,* V, 790–91), identifying this as paschal lamb imagery — in German, *das Oster-Lamm*. Both Olearius and Calov also cite here I Corinthians 5:7, "our paschal lamb, Christ, has been sacrificed." Luther, *Das 18. und 19. Kapitel,* 409: "he had to be the proper passover lamb" (*er hat sollen das rechte Osterlamb sein*). Therefore, the libretto's *ihm* should be understood as a neuter, not masculine, dative pronoun. John's Greek, *autou,* is ambiguous. It could be translated "its" or "his." Those who favor "his" might give up the paschal lamb imagery here and assume the scripture reference is to the persecuted psalmist of Psalm 34:21 (Brown, *Death of the Messiah,* 1185–86).

82. Zechariah 12:10 (Calov, *Die heilige Bibel,* V, 953; Olearius, *Biblische Erklärung,* V, 791).

83. See the discussion of this chorale on p. 34.

NR. 38 (66) REZITATIV
EVANGELIST

Darnach bat Pilatum Joseph von
Arimathia, der ein Jünger Jesu war
(doch heimlich, aus Furcht vor den
Jüden), daß er möchte abnehmen den
Leichnam Jesu. Und Pilatus erlaubete
es. Derowegen kam er und nahm den
Leichnam Jesu herab. Es kam aber auch
Nikodemus, der vormals bei der Nacht
zu Jesu kommen war, und brachte
Myrrhen und Aloen untereinander, bei
hundert Pfunden. Da nahmen sie den
Leichnam Jesu und bunden ihn in
leinen Tücher mit Spezereien, wie die
Jüden pflegen zu begraben. Es war aber
an der Stätte, da er gekreuziget ward,
ein Garte, und im Garten ein neu
Grab, in welches niemand je geleget
war. Daselbst hin legten sie Jesum, um
des Rüsttags willen der Jüden, dieweil
das Grab nahe war.

NO. 38 (66) RECITATIVE
EVANGELIST

After that, Joseph of Arimathea, who
was a disciple of Jesus (but secretly, for
fear of the Jews[84]*), asked Pilate that he*
might take down Jesus' corpse. And
Pilate allowed it. Consequently he
came and took down Jesus' corpse. But
there came also Nicodemus, who
formerly had come to Jesus by night,
and brought a mixture of myrrh and
aloes, about a hundred pounds.[85] *Then*
they took Jesus' corpse and bound it in
linen cloths with spices, the way the
Jews are accustomed to burying.[86] *But*
there was by the place where he was
crucified a garden, and in the garden a
new grave, in which nobody had ever
been laid. Right there they laid Jesus,
for the sake of the preparation day of
the Jews, because the grave was near.

84. The gospel's language suggests that a follower of Jesus is not a Jew, when in fact Jesus' first followers were Jews who also remained committed to the beliefs and practices of the religion of Judaism. Olearius, *Biblische Erklärung*, V, 791, comments here: "Jews who excommunicated all who confessed [Jesus as] Christ. John 9:22,34. See Isaiah 53:2–3." See the discussion of the expression "for fear of the Jews" on pp. 21–23; and n. 32 above in the present translation.

85. With echoes from the Hebrew Scriptures, the gospel is describing an honorable burial for a regal figure, culminating the triumph of Jesus' glorifying crucifixion (Brown, *Death of the Messiah*, 1260–70: Jeremiah 34:5; II Chronicles 16:14).

86. Calov commentary: "[for] their friends among the nobility" (*Die heilige Bibel*, V, 954); Olearius: Genesis 50 (*Biblische Erklärung*, V, 791).

NR. 39 (67) CHOR
Ruht wohl, ihr heiligen Gebeine,
Die ich nun weiter nicht beweine,
Ruht wohl und bringt auch mich zur
Ruh!
    Das Grab, so euch bestimmet ist
    Und ferner keine Not
      umschließt,
      Macht mir den Himmel auf und
      schließt die Hölle zu.

NO. 39 (67) CHORUS
Be fully at peace, you holy bones,[87]
which I will no longer bewail;
be fully at peace and bring also me to
this peace!
    The grave, so to you predestined
    and henceforth no distress will
      enclose,
      opens to me the [gates of]
      heaven and closes the [gates
      of] hell.

NR. 40 (68) CHORAL
Ach Herr, laß dein lieb Engelein
Am letzten End die Seele mein
In Abrahams Schoß tragen,
Den Leib in seim Schlafkämmerlein

Gar sanft, ohn einge Qual und Pein

Ruhn bis am jüngsten Tage!
Alsdenn vom Tod erwecke mich,
Daß meine Augen sehen dich
In aller Freud, o Gottes Sohn,
Mein Heiland und Genadenthron!
Herr Jesu Christ, erhöre mich,
Ich will dich preisen ewiglich!

NO. 40 (68) CHORALE
O Lord, let your dear angel
at the very end carry my soul
to Abraham's bosom;[88]
[let] my body in its little sleeping
    chamber,
completely in peace, without any
    tribulation and pain,
rest until the Last Day!
Then from death awaken me,
so that my eyes will behold you
in all joy, O Son of God,
my Saviour and Throne of Grace!
Lord Jesus Christ, grant me this;
I want to praise you for ever!

87. This is not simply a poem about Jesus' remains. It also refers to the church, the "body of Christ" — Jesus being the "head," his followers the "members" (see, e.g., I Corinthians 12:27–28). The images in *"Ruht wohl"* are developed extensively in Bach's Easter cantata *Der Himmel lacht! die Erde jubilieret* (BWV 31).

88. "Abraham's bosom" means "heaven." See, e.g., the language in the story of Lazarus and the rich man in Luke 16:22 (explained in Calov, *Die heilige Bibel*, V, 565).

Appendix 1

Notes on Anti-Judaism and Bach's Other Works

In giving lectures on Bach's *St. John Passion,* I have sometimes been asked to comment on anti-Judaism in Bach's other works. Renate Steiger has already published an important study on this question; I will simply summarize her discussion of the libretto of Bach's church cantata *Schauet doch und sehet, ob irgendein Schmerz sei* (BWV 46) and, with reference to Bach's biblical commentary by Johann Olearius, expand a bit on her discussion of the poetic commentary on Matthew 27:25 in Bach's *St. Matthew Passion.*[1]

Cantatas for the 10th Sunday after Trinity

Schauet doch und sehet is, so far as I know, Bach's only work that expresses contempt for contemporary Jews.[2] The cantata was written for the 10th Sunday after Trinity, whose specified gospel reading was Luke 19:41–48, where Jesus is depicted as predicting the destruction of Jerusalem and driving traders out of the Temple. In Leipzig it was the practice on this Sunday to read along with the pericope from Luke 19 the first-century historian Josephus's account of Titus's destruction of Jerusalem in 70 C.E.[3]

The opening chorus of Cantata 46 quotes verbatim Lamentations 1:12, poetry expressing sorrow over the destruction of Jerusalem and the Babylonian exile of its people in 586 B.C.E. There is a great deal of harsh commentary on this verse in the tenor recitative that follows. Its opening sentence, "So lament, you destroyed city of God, you wretched pile of stones and ashes! . . . You were handled like Gomorrah,[4] though not completely annihilated," refers to the historical situation of 70 C.E. — the notion that this second destruction of Jerusalem reflected God's judgment on the city

---

1. Steiger, "Bach und Israel," 21, for *Schauet doch;* 19–20, for Matthew 27:25 in the *St. Matthew Passion.* (Hoffmann-Axthelm, "Bach und die *perfidia Iudaica,*" does not cite this article.)

2. Concerning negative comments about Jews of Jesus' day in one of Bach's works, see n. 32 in the Annotated Literal Translation.

3. *Leipziger Kirchen-Staat,* 37. Incidentally, Bach owned a copy of Josephus, listed in his effects as "Josephi, *Geschichte der Jüden*" (Leaver, *Bachs Theologische Bibliothek,* 37).

4. See Genesis 19:24–28, where God is reported to have destroyed the cities of Sodom and Gomorrah because of their inhabitants' wickedness.

for its rejection of Jesus as Christ is expressed in the words, "You did not consider Jesus' tears; consider now then the zeal of the floodwaves that you have drawn upon yourself." This hostility is brought into the present, however, with the lines, "O better had you been destroyed to your foundations than that one now hear Christ's enemy blaspheming in you." (I would consider sophistical the objection that Jerusalem was a Muslim city in Bach's day.) The alto recitative goes on to bring judgment on Bach's Lutheran congregants as well: "But do not imagine, indeed, O sinners, it had been Jerusalem alone more than others [that] was filled with sins! . . . all of you may have to perish so horribly." It is unclear whether or not the differences between Christians and the literal "Jerusalem" are intensified in the words of the alto aria: "However, Jesus, even in punishment, wants to be the shield and assistance of the devout, . . . When storms of vengeance reward sinners, he helps, so that the devout live securely."

(Bach's other cantatas for the 10th Sunday after Trinity, *Nimm von uns, Herr, du treuer Gott* [BWV 101] and *Herr, deine Augen sehen nach dem Glauben* [BWV 102], generalize God's judgment and focus on Satan and "the world" as God's enemies.)

St. Matthew Passion

Lutheranism, anti-Judaism, and Bach's *St. Matthew Passion* is a subject worthy of an extended study. Suffice it generally to say here that the *St. Matthew Passion*'s commentaries on Matthew's passion narrative place a much greater emphasis on the guilt of Protestant Christians than does the *St. John Passion*'s on John's. Also, Matthew's narrative more clearly directs its negativity at the Jewish leaders than at a broader if arguably multivalent category like John's *hoi Ioudaioi* ("the Jews"). For this reason, I will focus only on the verse that has engendered the greatest curiosity from my lecture audiences, Matthew 27:25, where, in response to Pilate's declaration of his own innocence in condemning Jesus, "all the people" are depicted as exclaiming, "His [Jesus'] blood be on us and our children."

A strictly literal translation of the gospel's Greek would read, "His blood on us and our children."[5] (There is no verb in Matthew's formula.) The biblical scholar Raymond Brown notes: "It is not wrong to supply a verb ('come' or 'be'), as many translations do; but that creates the danger of misreading the phrase as a self-curse, a prophecy, or a blood-thirsty wish"[6] (which have been in fact the most common ways of reading the verse). The

---

5. Brown, *Death of the Messiah,* 837.
6. Brown, *Death of the Messiah,* 837.

way Luther Bibles, and therefore Bach's *St. Matthew Passion,* give the passage is: *Sein Blut komme über uns und unsre Kinder* ("his blood come over us and our children"). Bach would have been familiar with interpretations that took the phrase to be a self-curse.[7] But as Steiger was the first to point out, Bach's *St. Matthew Passion* reads the phrase differently, waiting until after verse 26 (the scourging of Jesus by the Roman soldiers) to break the biblical narrative with commentary.[8] The *St. Matthew Passion* meditates not on the responsibility of "the [Jewish] people" for Jesus' crucifixion but on the redemptive power of "his blood." The text of the alto aria *"Können Tränen meiner Wangen"* reads, "let [my heart] at the streaming, when the wounds abundantly[9] bleed, even be the sacrificial cup!"

Steiger notes that the validity of her observations is not jeopardized by the fact that the sermon literature Bach had at his disposal did not provide this exegetical tack.[10] I would like to suggest however, that it was Bach's biblical commentary by Olearius that could have been a source for Bach and his librettist, Christian Friedrich Henrici (also known as Picander), in producing this redemptive reading for the *St. Matthew Passion.*[11]

Olearius suggests that Matthew 27:25 is bivalent. It connotes judgment and redemption. He writes concerning the verse:

> *His blood; NB.* Genesis 4. Matthew 23:35. [About] this blood-guilt *NB.* Psalm 51:16; together with every curse, threat, and punishment — about this *NB.* Genesis 27:13; about this Lamentations 5:7 . . . *come over us;* about this *NB.* Genesis 27:13. [As if to say:] "Do this upon our own responsibility; we want to indemnify you. Let it come on our children and descendants. Should it happen to him unjustly, then we want to carry the guilt." At which [it is] worth remembering: . . . 2. The horrible fulfillment after 40 years . . . 3. The comforting conversion of this curse into blessing. For the power of the blood of Jesus Christ comes over us, and purifies us; 1 John 1, that is to say: "Your goodness be over us," Psalm 33:22, which is redemption for the many. *NB.* Psalm 130:7.[12]

Notice that Genesis 27:13 figures in Olearius's comments both on judgment and on redemption. Concerning this verse (where Rebekah replies

---

7. For example, Calov, *Die heilige Bibel,* V, 284: "This was a horrible curse, through which they have precipitately incurred and drawn upon themselves and their entire lineage not only temporal but also eternal vengeance, expulsion, and damnation. Of the like example, as also of such a true vengeance, among no people from the outset of the world is [there] to [be] read."

8. Steiger, "Bach und Israel," 19–20.

9. On the translation of *milde* as "abundantly," not "calmly" or "gently," see n. 62 in the Annotated Literal Translation.

10. Steiger, "Bach und Israel," 20, n. 24.

11. Bach and Picander possibly collaborated on the theological content of Picander's poetry in the *St. Matthew Passion,* for the libretto draws on material from the passion sermons of Heinrich Müller in Bach's library. See Axmacher, "Ein Quellenfund," 181–91.

12. Olearius, *Biblische Erklärung,* V, 252.

"the curse be on me" to her son Jacob's worry that if he goes to his blind father Isaac pretending to be his older brother Esau, he will bring on himself a curse instead of the hoped-for fatherly blessing from the Lord of the first born), Olearius writes:

> [Rebekah said, "Let the curse] come over me; it meet me and remain on me." So said the Jews: "his blood come over us," namely the punishment of the innocent blood. Matthew 27:25. [Rebekah] said ["the curse be on me"] to convince Jacob, for she knew assuredly that here there was not a curse to face but a blessing. So says also David, Psalm 33:22. Your goodness, Lord, be over us, as a steadfast protection, *NB*. Psalm 91:1–2, and remain over us unchangingly.[13]

At his commentary on Genesis 27:13, Calov writes something similar:

> [Rebekah] said ["the curse be on me"] out of assured trust that it would turn out such that Jacob would receive not a curse but a beautiful fatherly blessing, at which she also could be delighted — which ascertainment originated from God's answer [to Rebekah in Genesis] 25:23.[14]

Now at his commentary on Psalm 33:22 ("Your goodness, Lord, be over us, as a steadfast protection"), Olearius writes:

> *Be over us* truly and remain steadfast, *NB*. Genesis 27:13. Matthew 27:25.[15]

Christians take the redemptive power of "his blood" to have been instituted by the words Jesus is depicted as saying in Matthew 26:27–28, words that Bach powerfully set in the *St. Matthew Passion* ("Drink from it, all [of you]; this is my blood of the new[16] covenant, which is shed for many for the forgiveness of sins").[17] At his commentary on Matthew 26:28, Olearius writes:

> *Blood; haima;* about this 1 John 1:7. This is ratification of the new covenant through my own blood . . . thus corresponding to the sacrificial blood [of] Exodus 24:8.[18]

At his commentary on Exodus 24:8 ("Then Moses took the [sacrificial] blood and sprinkled the people with it, and exclaimed, 'Behold, this is the blood of the covenant that the Lord [has] made with you . . .'"), Olearius writes:

---

13. Olearius, *Biblische Erklärung*, I/2, 208.

14. Calov, *Die heilige Bibel*, I, 202. The first "X" in "XXV.23" has been corrected by hand (by Bach?) in Bach's own copy of Calov (this page is not reproduced in Cox, *Calov Bible*).

15. Olearius, *Biblische Erklärung*, III, 208.

16. Many recent translations of Matthew read "this is my blood of the covenant." The word "new" was added to 26:28 in some early manuscripts of Matthew (the same is true for Mark 14:24) and reproduced in Luther's translation.

17. The biblical narrative within Bach's *St. Matthew Passion* includes Luther's translation of chapters 26 and 27 of Matthew.

18. Olearius, *Biblische Erklärung*, V, 230.

Blood of the covenant; Dam habberith; about this Leviticus 26 and Nehemiah 9, whose Mosaic covenant of law corresponds to the gospel covenant of grace and the blood of Jesus Christ in the New Testament. Matthew 26. Hebrews 9:19.[19]

Taking a blessing to appear behind a curse happens again toward the end of Bach's *St. Matthew Passion,* at the aria *"Ach Golgotha,"* whose third and fourth lines read, "the blessing and salvation of the world appears on the cross as a curse."[20]

I hope these observations will serve to bolster Steiger's conclusion that fostering hostility to Jews is not the subject or purpose of the commentary on Matthew's passion narrative in Bach's *St. Matthew Passion.*[21]

19. Olearius, *Biblische Erklärung,* I/2, 496.

20. See the similar linking of curse with blessing in Bach's church cantatas *Herr, wie du willt, so schicks mit mir* (BWV 73) and *Jesu, der du meine Seele* (BWV 78).

21. Steiger, "Bach und Israel," 20. That the seventeenth-century German Lutheran composer Heinrich Schütz's music projects a redemptive view of Matthew 27:25 is argued in Marti, "Heil oder Gericht? Das Blut Christi," 145–49. For modern biblical scholarship arguing a redemptive interpretation, see Brown, *Death of the Messiah,* 839; and Levine, *Social and Ethnic Dimensions of Matthean Salvation History,* 268–69 (Brown and Levine also indicate the plausibility of other, more negative interpretations). Levine suggests a literary connection between Matthew 27:25 and the institution of the Eucharist in 26:28, and she goes on to say that "the promise made at the beginning of the gospel that Jesus would 'save his people from their sins' (1:21) is recapitulated by these same people [in 27:25]. The crowd has, in very ironic circumstances, bestowed a blessing upon itself and its offspring."

Appendix 2

Musical Examples

Selected Bach *St. John Passion* recordings

Frans Brüggen, Netherlands Chamber Choir, Orchestra of the 18th Century; Philips 434 905-2 (Philips Classics Productions, 1993).

John Eliot Gardiner, The Monteverdi Choir, The English Baroque Soloists; Archiv Produktion 419 324-2 (Polydor International GmbH Hamburg, 1986).

Nikolaus Harnoncourt, Wiener Sängerknaben, Chorus Viennensis, Concentus musicus Wien; Teldec — *Das alte Werk* 2292-42492-2 (Teldec Schallplatten, 1987; orig. 1971).

Nikolaus Harnoncourt, Arnold Schoenberg Chor, Concentus musicus Wien; Teldec — *Das alte Werk* 9031-74862-2 (Teldec Classics International GmbH Hamburg, 1995).

Ton Koopman, Koor van de Nederlandse Bachvereniging, The Amsterdam Baroque Orchestra; Erato 4509-94675-2 (Erato Disques S.A., 1994).

Sigiswald Kuijken, Choir and Orchestra of *La petite Bande;* deutsche harmonia mundia — editio classica 77041-2-RG (BMG Music, 1990; orig. 1988).

Helmuth Rilling, Gächinger Kantorei Stuttgart, Bach-Collegium Stuttgart; hänssler classic — Exclusive Series, CD 98.170 (Hänssler-Verlag, Neuhausen-Stuttgart, 1997) (includes movements from all versions; features spoken commentary in English by Helmuth Rilling).

Kenneth Slowik, The Smithsonian Chamber Chorus, The Smithsonian Chamber Players; *The Smithsonian Collection of Recordings* ND 0381 (Smithsonian Institution, 1990) (includes two choruses and three arias from the 1725 version).

Ex. 1, no. 1, measures 1–25

Brüggen	CD 1	track 1	0:00–1:39
Gardiner	CD 1	track 1	0:00–1:33
Harnoncourt 1971	CD 1	track 1	0:00–1:44
Harnoncourt 1995	CD 1	track 1	0:00–1:32
Koopman	CD 1	track 1	0:00–1:38
Kuijken	CD 1	track 1	0:00–1:27
Rilling	CD 1	track 1	0:00–1:19
Slowik	CD 1	track 1	0:00–1:24

Ex. 2, no. 2c, measures 22–23

Brüggen	CD 1	track 2	1:12–1:20
Gardiner	CD 1	track 2	1:10–1:18
Harnoncourt 1971	CD 1	track 4	0:00–0:08
Harnoncourt 1995	CD 1	track 2	1:20–1:28
Koopman	CD 1	track 4	0:00–0:06
Kuijken	CD 1	track 4	0:00–0:07
Rilling	CD 1	track 2	1:27–1:35
Slowik	CD 1	track 2	1:06–1:13

Ex. 3, no. 18a, measures 1–5

Brüggen	CD 1	track 18	0:00–0:18
Gardiner	CD 1	track 18	0:00–0:19
Harnoncourt 1971	CD 1	track 28	0:00–0:21
Harnoncourt 1995	CD 2	track 4	0:00–0:20
Koopman	CD 1	track 28	0:00–0:18
Kuijken	CD 1	track 27	0:00–0:21
Rilling	CD 1	track 18	0:00–0:28
Slowik	CD 1	track 18	0:00–0:16

Ex. 4, no. 16a, measures 7–10

Brüggen	CD 1	track 16	0:24–0:37
Gardiner	CD 1	track 16	0:22–0:30
Harnoncourt 1971	CD 1	track 22	0:21–0:33
Harnoncourt 1995	CD 2	track 2	0:20–0:32
Koopman	CD 1	track 22	0:20–0:31
Kuijken	CD 1	track 21	0:21–0:34
Rilling	CD 1	track 16	0:33–0:44
Slowik	CD 1	track 16	0:19–0:29

Ex. 5, no. 16c, measures 39–41

Brüggen	CD 1	track 16	1:33–1:44
Gardiner	CD 1	track 16	1:37–1:47
Harnoncourt 1971	CD 1	track 24	0:00–0:10
Harnoncourt 1995	CD 2	track 2	1:40–1:52
Koopman	CD 1	track 24	0:00–0:09
Kuijken	CD 1	track 23	0:00–0:09
Rilling	CD 1	track 16	1:54–2:04
Slowik	CD 1	track 16	1:31–1:41

Ex. 6, no. 18a, measures 13–17

Brüggen	CD 1	track 18	1:00–1:16
Gardiner	CD 1	track 18	0:54–1:11
Harnoncourt 1971	CD 1	track 28	1:02–1:17
Harnoncourt 1995	CD 2	track 4	1:02–1:14
Koopman	CD 1	track 28	0:55–1:11
Kuijken	CD 1	track 27	1:02–1:18
Rilling	CD 1	track 18	1:19–1:36
Slowik	CD 1	track 18	0:53–1:10

Ex. 7, no. 16e, measures 66–70

Brüggen	CD 1	track 16	2:50–3:10
Gardiner	CD 1	track 16	2:53–3:09
Harnoncourt 1971	CD 1	track 26	0:27–0:48
Harnoncourt 1995	CD 2	track 2	3:06–3:25
Koopman	CD 1	track 26	0:27–0:46
Kuijken	CD 1	track 25	0:31–0:48
Rilling	CD 1	track 16	3:18–3:39
Slowik	CD 1	track 16	2:46–3:03

Ex. 8, no. 21b, measures 5–16

Brüggen	CD 2	track 1	0:18–0:51
Gardiner	CD 2	track 1	0:16–0:50
Harnoncourt 1971	CD 1	track 34	0:00–0:31
Harnoncourt 1995	CD 2	track 7	0:16–0:55
Koopman	CD 1	track 34	0:00–0:32
Kuijken	CD 2	track 2	0:00–0:34
Rilling	CD 2	track 1	0:21–0:56
Slowik	CD 2	track 1	0:16–0:50

Ex. 9, no. 9, measures 17–28

Brüggen	CD 1	track 9	0:20–0:37
Gardiner	CD 1	track 9	0:19–0:34
Harnoncourt 1971	CD 1	track 13	0:25–0:44
Harnoncourt 1995	CD 1	track 9	0:24–0:42
Koopman	CD 1	track 13	0:19–0:35
Kuijken	CD 1	track 12	0:21–0:39
Rilling	CD 1	track 9	0:20–0:36
Slowik	CD 1	track 9	0:20–0:36

Ex. 10, no. 8, measures 1–3

Brüggen	CD 1	track 8	0:00–0:13
Gardiner	CD 1	track 8	0:00–0:13
Harnoncourt 1971	CD 1	track 12	0:00–0:12
Harnoncourt 1995	CD 1	track 8	0:00–0:12
Koopman	CD 1	track 12	0:00–0:10
Kuijken	CD 1	track 11	0:00–0:11
Rilling	CD 1	track 8	0:00–0:19
Slowik	CD 1	track 8	0:00–0:12

Ex. 11, no. 10, measures 13–15

Brüggen	CD 1	track 10	0:44–0:56
Gardiner	CD 1	track 10	0:37–0:48
Harnoncourt 1971	CD 1	track 14	0:39–0:51
Harnoncourt 1995	CD 1	track 10	0:40–0:53
Koopman	CD 1	track 14	0:37–0:47
Kuijken	CD 1	track 13	0:43–0:56
Rilling	CD 1	track 10	0:52–1:05
Slowik	CD 1	track 10	0:39–0:49

Ex. 12, no. 9, measures 153–56

Brüggen	CD 1	track 9	3:28–3:36
Gardiner	CD 1	track 9	3:03–3:10
Harnoncourt 1971	CD 1	track 13	4:04–4:11
Harnoncourt 1995	CD 1	track 9	3:54–4:03
Koopman	CD 1	track 13	3:20–3:27
Kuijken	CD 1	track 12	3:36–3:42
Rilling	CD 1	track 9	3:19–3:25
Slowik	CD 1	track 9	3:17–3:24

Ex. 13, no. 13, measures 17–24

Brüggen	CD 1	track 13	0:25–0:38
Gardiner	CD 1	track 13	0:24–0:36
Harnoncourt 1971	CD 1	track 19	0:26–0:40
Harnoncourt 1995	CD 1	track 13	0:26–0:39
Koopman	CD 1	track 19	0:27–0:41
Kuijken	CD 1	track 18	0:29–0:43
Rilling	CD 1	track 13	0:26–0:38
Slowik	CD 1	track 13	0:25–0:38

Ex. 14, no. 30, measures 1–7

Brüggen	CD 2	track 10	0:00–1:25
Gardiner	CD 2	track 10	0:00–1:18
Harnoncourt 1971	CD 2	track 18	0:00–1:09
Harnoncourt 1995	CD 2	track 16	0:00–1:15
Koopman	CD 2	track 18	0:00–1:17
Kuijken	CD 2	track 26	0:00–1:29
Rilling	CD 2	track 10	0:00–1:29
Slowik	CD 2	track 10	0:00–1:21

Ex. 15, no. 30, measures 17–34

Brüggen	CD 2	track 10	3:33–4:27
Gardiner	CD 2	track 10	3:13–4:00
Harnoncourt 1971	CD 2	track 18	3:04–4:02
Harnoncourt 1995	CD 2	track 16	3:01–3:50
Koopman	CD 2	track 18	3:09–3:57
Kuijken	CD 2	track 26	3:46–4:42
Rilling	CD 2	track 10	3:43–4:36
Slowik	CD 2	track 10	3:18–4:10

Ex. 16, no. 30, measures 32–41

Brüggen	CD 2	track 10	4:23–4:52
Gardiner	CD 2	track 10	3:57–4:27
Harnoncourt 1971	CD 2	track 18	3:58–4:29
Harnoncourt 1995	CD 2	track 16	3:45–4:17
Koopman	CD 2	track 18	3:54–4:25
Kuijken	CD 2	track 26	4:38–5:13
Rilling	CD 2	track 10	4:33–5:08
Slowik	CD 2	track 10	4:06–4:38

Ex. 17, no. 29, measures 11–14

Brüggen	CD 2	track 9	0:50–1:22
Gardiner	CD 2	track 9	0:48–1:15
Harnoncourt 1971	CD 2	track 17	0:46–1:17
Harnoncourt 1995	CD 2	track 15	0:49–1:14
Koopman	CD 2	track 17	0:49–1:16
Kuijken	CD 2	track 25	0:45–1:15
Rilling	CD 2	track 9	1:01–1:41
Slowik	CD 2	track 9	0:58–1:26

Ex. 18, no. 30, measures 42–44

Brüggen	CD 2	track 10	5:09–5:45
Gardiner	CD 2	track 10	4:43–5:16
Harnoncourt 1971	CD 2	track 18	4:45–5:14
Harnoncourt 1995	CD 2	track 16	4:34–5:05
Koopman	CD 2	track 18	4:42–5:13
Kuijken	CD 2	track 26	5:32–6:09
Rilling	CD 2	track 10	5:28–6:04
Slowik	CD 2	track 10	4:54–5:24

Ex. 19, no. 21f, measures 57–69

Brüggen	CD 2	track 1	2:52–3:16
Gardiner	CD 2	track 1	2:51–3:18
Harnoncourt 1971	CD 1	track 38	0:00–0:24
Harnoncourt 1995	CD 2	track 7	3:16–3:44
Koopman	CD 1	track 38	0:00–0:25
Kuijken	CD 2	track 6	0:00–0:28
Rilling	CD 2	track 1	3:15–3:44
Slowik	CD 2	track 1	2:56–3:22

Ex. 20, no. 37, measures 1–17

Brüggen	CD 2	track 17	0:00–0:56
Gardiner	CD 2	track 17	0:00–1:01
Harnoncourt 1971	CD 2	track 25	0:00–1:07
Harnoncourt 1995	CD 2	track 23	0:00–0:56
Koopman	CD 2	track 25	0:00–0:57
Kuijken	CD 2	track 33	0:00–1:16
Rilling	CD 2	track 17	0:00–1:10
Slowik	CD 2	track 17	0:00–1:00

Ex. 21, no. 11, the repeat of measures 1–12

Brüggen	CD 1	track 11	0:42–1:25
Gardiner	CD 1	track 11	0:42–1:30
Harnoncourt 1971	CD 1	track 15	0:52–1:47
Harnoncourt 1995	CD 1	track 11	0:47–1:34
Koopman	CD 1	track 15	0:43–1:30
Kuijken	CD 1	track 14	1:04–2:13
Rilling	CD 1	track 11	0:49–1:41
Slowik	CD 1	track 11	0:46–1:37

Ex. 22, no. 10, measures 25–37

Brüggen	CD 1	track 10	1:34–2:29
Gardiner	CD 1	track 10	1:22–2:06
Harnoncourt 1971	CD 1	track 14	1:28–2:21
Harnoncourt 1995	CD 1	track 10	1:32–2:23
Koopman	CD 1	track 14	1:22–2:13
Kuijken	CD 1	track 13	1:34–2:22
Rilling	CD 1	track 10	2:00–3:00
Slowik	CD 1	track 10	1:21–2:12

Ex. 23, no. 21g, measures 99–102

Brüggen	CD 2	track 1	4:42–4:57
Gardiner	CD 2	track 1	4:45–4:56
Harnoncourt 1971	CD 1	track 39	0:34–0:51
Harnoncourt 1995	CD 2	track 7	5:13–5:27
Koopman	CD 1	track 39	0:36–0:51
Kuijken	CD 2	track 7	0:44–1:02
Rilling	CD 2	track 1	5:33–5:47
Slowik	CD 2	track 1	4:46–5:01

Works Cited

Adelung, Johann Christoph. *Grammatisch-kritisches Wörterbuch der Hoch-deutschen Mundart.* Rev. ed. Leipzig, 1793.

Agenda: Das ist Kirchen-Ordnung, Wie sich die Pfarrherren und Seelsorger in ihren Aemtern und Diensten verhalten sollen; Für die Diener der Kirchen in . . . Sachsen. Leipzig, 1712; orig. 1540.
This *Saxon Agenda* went through a large number of reprintings between the sixteenth and eighteenth centuries. The 1712 edition was the one used in Leipzig during Bach's tenure there (see Stiller, *Johann Sebastian Bach and Liturgical Life,* 36); the 1712 version was reprinted, keeping its own pagination, in the *Vollständiges Kirchen-Buch* of 1731.

Aland, Kurt. *Hilfsbuch zum Lutherstudium.* Rev. ed. Witten: Luther-Verlag, 1970.

Aulén, Gustaf. *Christus Victor: An Historical Study of the Three Main Types of the Idea of the Atonement,* trans. A. G. Hebert. New York: Macmillan, 1961; orig. 1931; Swedish orig. 1930; German ed. 1930.

Axmacher, Elke. *"Aus Liebe will mein Heiland Sterben": Untersuchungen zum Wandel des Passionsverständnisses im frühen 18. Jahrhundert.* Neuhausen-Stuttgart: Hänssler, 1984.

———. "Ein Quellenfund zum Text der Matthäus-Passion." *Bach-Jahr-buch* 64 (1978): 181–91.

Beißwenger, Kirsten. *Johann Sebastian Bachs Notenbibliothek.* Cassel: Bären-reiter, 1992.

Brockes, Barthold Heinrich. *Der für die Sünde der Welt gemarterte und Sterbende Jesus.* Hamburg, 1712; rev. 1713.

Brown, Raymond E. *The Death of the Messiah: A Commentary on the Passion Narratives in the Four Gospels.* New York: Doubleday, 1994.
This is an indispensable and formidable piece of work. For a briefer treatment of its themes, see Brown, "Narratives." Although the book has received many positive reviews, its methods have also been questioned, technically and even

ethically. See, e.g., Crossan's incisive review in *Journal of Religion* 75 (1995): 247–53, and his *Who Killed Jesus?* See also Pagels, *Origin of Satan,* passim.

———. *An Introduction to New Testament Christology.* New York: Paulist Press, 1994.

———. "The Narratives of Jesus' Passion and Anti-Judaism." *America* 172, no. 11 (1995): 8–12.

Calov, Abraham. *Die heilige Bibel nach S. Herrn D. Martini Lutheri Deutscher Dolmetschung und Erklärung.* Wittenberg, 1681–82.
Bach's copy, with his numerous highlightings and marginal comments, is housed at Concordia Seminary Library, St. Louis.

Chafe, Eric. *Tonal Allegory in the Vocal Music of J. S. Bach.* Berkeley and Los Angeles: University of California Press, 1991.

Cox, Howard H., ed. *The Calov Bible of J. S. Bach.* Ann Arbor: UMI Research Press, 1985.

Crossan, John Dominic. *Who Killed Jesus?: Exposing the Roots of Anti-Semitism in the Gospel Story of the Death of Jesus.* San Francisco: HarperSanFrancisco, 1995.

David, Hans T., and Arthur Mendel, eds. *The Bach Reader: A Life of Johann Sebastian Bach in Letters and Documents.* Rev. ed. New York: Norton, 1966.

Dershowitz, Alan. *Chutzpah.* Boston: Little, Brown, 1991.

Dreyfus, Laurence. "J. S. Bach and the Status of Genre: Problems of Style in the G-minor Sonata BWV 1029." *Journal of Musicology* 5 (1987): 55–78. Rev. as "The Status of a Genre," in Dreyfus, *Bach and the Patterns of Invention,* 103–33. Cambridge, Mass.: Harvard University Press, 1996.

Dürr, Alfred. *Die Johannes-Passion von Johann Sebastian Bach: Entstehung, Überlieferung, Werkeinführung.* Munich and Cassel: dtv/Bärenreiter, 1988.

———. *Die Kantaten von Johann Sebastian Bach.* Munich and Cassel: dtv/Bärenreiter, 1988; orig. 1971.

Edwards, Jr., Mark U. *Luther's Last Battles: Politics and Polemics, 1531–46.* Ithaca: Cornell University Press, 1983.

Evans, C. Stephen. *The Historical Christ and the Jesus of Faith: The Incarnational Narrative as History.* Oxford: Clarendon Press, 1996.

Finke-Hecklinger, Doris. *Tanzcharaktere in Johann Sebastian Bachs Vokalmusik.* Trossingen: Hohner, 1970.

Franklin, Don O. "The Libretto of Bach's John Passion and the Doctrine of Reconciliation: An Historical Perspective." In *Das Blut Jesu und die Lehre von der Versöhnung im Werk Johann Sebastian Bachs,* ed. A. A. Clement, 179–203. Amsterdam: North-Holland, 1995.

Fredriksen, Paula. *From Jesus to Christ: The Origins of the New Testament Images of Jesus.* New Haven: Yale University Press, 1988.

Friedman, Jerome. "Antisemitism." In *The Oxford Encyclopedia of the Reformation,* ed. Hans J. Hillerbrand, vol. 1, 53–55. New York: Oxford University Press, 1996.

Geck, Martin. *Johann Sebastian Bach: Johannespassion BWV 245.* Munich: Fink, 1991.

Herz, Gerhard. "J. S. Bach 1733: A 'New' Bach Signature." In *Studies in Renaissance and Baroque Music in Honor of Arthur Mendel,* ed. Robert L. Marshall, 255–63. Cassel: Bärenreiter, 1974.

Heschel, Susannah. "Nazifying Christian Theology: Walter Grundmann and the Institute for the Study and Eradication of Jewish Influence on German Church Life." *Church History* 63 (1994): 587–605.

Hillerbrand, Hans J. "Martin Luther and the Jews." In *Jews and Christians: Exploring the Past, Present, and Future,* ed. James H. Charlesworth, 127–50. New York: Crossroad, 1990.

Hoffmann-Axthelm, Dagmar. "Bach und die *perfidia Iudaica:* Zur Symmetrie der Juden-Turbae in der Johannes-Passion." *Basler Jahrbuch für historische Musikpraxis* 13 (1989): 31–54.

Holstein, Hugo. *Die Reformation im Spiegelbilde der dramatischen Litteratur des sechzehnten Jahrhunderts.* Nieuwkoop: B. de Graaf, 1967; orig. 1886.

Horbury, William. "The Benediction of the *Minim* and Early Jewish-Christian Controversy." *Journal of Theological Studies* 33 (1982): 19–61.

Horsley, Richard. "High Priests and the Politics of Roman Palestine: A Contextual Analysis of the Evidence in Josephus." *Journal for the Study of Judaism* 17 (1986): 23–55.

Hutter, Leonard. *Compend of Lutheran Theology,* trans. H. E. Jacobs and G. F. Spieker. Philadelphia: The Lutheran Book Store, 1868; Latin orig. 1609.
German trans. 1610, and German trans. by Hutter 1611; thereafter numerous reprintings from the seventeenth to nineteenth centuries (Jacobs' preface, v).

Jenne, Natalie, and Meredith Little. *Dance and the Music of J. S. Bach.* Bloomington: Indiana University Press, 1991.

Käsemann, Ernst. *The Testament of Jesus: A Study of the Gospel of John in Light of Chapter 17,* trans. Gerhard Krodel. Philadelphia: Fortress, 1968; German orig. 1966.

Kimelman, Reuven. "*Birkat Ha-Minim* and the Lack of Evidence for an Anti-Christian Jewish Prayer in Late Antiquity." In *Jewish and Christian Self-Definition,* vol. 2, *Aspects of Judaism in the Graeco-Roman Period,* ed. E. P. Sanders et al., 226–44, 391–403. Philadelphia: Fortress, 1981.

Klenicki, Leon, ed. *Passion Plays and Judaism.* New York: Anti-Defamation League, 1996.
This publication is available from the Anti-Defamation League of B'nai B'rith, Department of Interfaith Affairs, 823 United Nations Plaza, New York, N.Y. 10017.

Klenicki, Leon, and Franklin Sherman. "Luther and Lutheranism on the Jews and Judaism: A Dialogue between Rabbi Leon Klenicki and Dr. Franklin Sherman." *Interfaith Focus* 2, no. 1 (1995): 1–18.
This publication is available from the address indicated under the previous entry.

Kreutzer, Hans Joachim. "Johann Sebastian Bach und das literarische Leipzig der Aufklärung." *Bach-Jahrbuch* 77 (1991): 7–31.

Kusko, Bruce. "Proton Milloprobe Analysis of the Hand-Penned Annotations in Bach's Calov Bible." In *The Calov Bible of J. S. Bach,* ed. Howard H. Cox, 31–106. Ann Arbor: UMI Research Press, 1985.

Langmuir, Gavin I. "Toward a Definition of Antisemitism." In Langmuir, *Toward a Definition of Antisemitism,* 311–52, 398–400. Berkeley and Los Angeles: University of California Press, 1990.

Leaver, Robin A. *Bachs Theologische Bibliothek: Eine kritische Bibliographie / Bach's Theological Library: A Critical Bibliography.* Neuhausen-Stuttgart: Hänssler, 1985.

————. *J. S. Bach as Preacher: His Passions and Music in Worship.* St. Louis: Concordia, 1984.

Leipziger Kirchen-Staat: Das ist Deutlicher Unterricht vom Gottes-Dienst in Leipzig . . . Nebst darauff eingerichteten Andächtigen Gebeten und . . . Gesängen. Leipzig, 1710.

Leisinger, Ulrich. "Forms and Functions of the Choral Movements in J. S. Bach's *St. Matthew Passion.*" In *Bach-Studies 2,* ed. Daniel R. Melamed, 70–84. Cambridge: Cambridge University Press, 1995.

Levenson, Jon D. *The Death and Resurrection of the Beloved Son: The Transformation of Child Sacrifice in Judaism and Christianity.* New Haven: Yale University Press, 1993.

Levine, Amy-Jill. *The Social and Ethnic Dimensions of Matthean Salvation History: "Go nowhere among the Gentiles . . ." (Matt. 10:5b).* Lewiston: Mellen, 1988.

Lindberg, Carter. "Tainted Greatness: Luther's Attitudes toward Judaism and Their Historical Reception." In *Tainted Greatness: Antisemitism and Cultural Heroes,* ed. Nancy A. Harrowitz, 15–35. Philadelphia: Temple University Press, 1994.

Little, Meredith, and Natalie Jenne. *Dance and the Music of J. S. Bach.* Bloomington: Indiana University Press, 1991.

Luther, Martin. *Das 18. und 19. Kapitel und ein Stück aus dem 20. S. Johannis von dem Leiden, Sterben und Auferstehung Jesu Christi,* ed. Paul Pietsch. In *D. Martin Luthers Werke: Kritische Gesamtausgabe,* vol. 28, 201–464. Weimar: Böhlau, 1903.
Bach owned copies of each of the Luther items listed here. One can determine which Luther works Bach had by collating information from Aland, *Hilfsbuch zum Lutherstudium,* and Leaver, *Bachs Theologische Bibliothek.*

————. *Hauspostille:* "Passio, oder Histori vom leyden Christi Jesu, unsers Heylands — 'Die Zwölfft Predig: Wie der Herr Christus seine mutter . . . aus dem Euangelio Johannis am xix,'" ed. Karl Drescher. In *D. Martin Luthers Werke: Kritische Gesamtausgabe,* vol. 52, 809–19. Weimar: Böhlau, 1915.

————. *Luther's Works,* vol. 25, *Lectures on Romans,* trans. Walter G. Tillmanns and Jacob A. O. Preus, ed. Hilton C. Oswald. St. Louis: Concordia, 1972.

————. *Luthers geistliche Lieder und Kirchengesänge: Vollständige Neuedition in Ergänzung zu Band 35 der Weimarer Ausgabe,* ed. Markus Jenny. Cologne: Böhlau, 1985.

————. "A Meditation on Christ's Passion, 1519." In *Luther's Works,* vol. 42, *Devotional Writings I,* trans. Martin H. Bertram, ed. Martin O. Dietrich, 3–14. Philadelphia: Fortress, 1969.

————. "On the Jews and their Lies, 1543," in *Luther's Works,* vol. 47, *The Christian in Society IV,* trans. Martin H. Bertram, ed. Franklin Sherman, 123–306. Philadelphia: Fortress, 1971.

————. *Luther's Works,* vol. 23, *Sermons on the Gospel of John, Chapters 6–8,* trans. Martin H. Bertram, ed. Jaroslav Pelikan and Daniel E. Poellot. St. Louis: Concordia, 1959.

Marissen, Michael. "Religious Aims in Mendelssohn's 1829 Berlin-Singakademie Performances of Bach's *St. Matthew Passion.*" *Musical Quarterly* 77 (1993): 718–26.

————. *The Social and Religious Designs of J. S. Bach's Brandenburg Concertos.* Princeton: Princeton University Press, 1995.

————. "The Theological Character of J. S. Bach's *Musical Offering.*" In *Bach-Studies 2,* ed. Daniel R. Melamed, 85–106. Cambridge: Cambridge University Press, 1995.

Markgraf, Richard. *Zur Geschichte der Juden auf den Messen in Leipzig von 1664–1839: Ein Beitrag zur Geschichte Leipzigs.* Bischofswerda, 1894.

Marpurg, Friedrich Wilhelm. *Anleitung zur Singekomposition.* Berlin, 1758.

Marshall, Robert L. "Tempo and Dynamics: The Original Terminology" (orig. 1985). In Marshall, *The Music of Johann Sebastian Bach: The Sources, the Style, the Significance,* 255–69, 333–37. New York: Schirmer, 1989.

Marti, Andreas. "Heil oder Gericht? Das Blut Christi in zwei Werken von Heinrich Schütz." In *Ars et Musica in Liturgia: Essays Presented to Casper Honders on His Seventieth Birthday,* ed. Robin A. Leaver, 145–49. Metuchen: Scarecrow, 1994.

Marty, Martin E. "Art that Offends." *Christian Century* 112 (1995): 351.

Martyn, J. Louis. *History and Theology in the Fourth Gospel.* Rev. and enl. ed. Nashville: Abington, 1979; orig. 1968.

McGrath, Alister E. *Luther's Theology of the Cross: Martin Luther's Theological Breakthrough.* Oxford: Blackwell, 1985.

Mendel, Arthur, ed. *Johann Sebastian Bach, Neue Ausgabe sämtlicher Werke* [*Neue Bach-Ausgabe*], series II, vol. 4, *Johannes-Passion.* Cassel: Bärenreiter, 1973–74.

Mendel, Arthur, and Hans T. David, ed. *The Bach Reader: A Life of Johann Sebastian Bach in Letters and Documents.* Rev. ed. New York: Norton, 1966.

Michael, Wolfgang F. "Luther and the Religious Drama." *Daphnis: Zeitschrift für Mittlere Deutsche Literatur* 7 (1978): 365–67.

Müller, Johannes. *Judaismus oder Jüdenthum — Das ist: Ausführlicher Bericht Von des Jüdischen Volcks Unglauben, Blindheit und Verstockung.* Hamburg, 1644.
Bach owned a copy of a 1707 edition (Leaver, *Bachs Theologische Bibliothek,* 116).

Nestle, Rosmarie. "Das Bachschrifttum 1981 bis 1985." *Bach-Jahrbuch* 75 (1989): 107–89.

———. "Das Bachschrifttum 1986 bis 1990." *Bach-Jahrbuch* 80 (1994): 75–162.

Netanyahu, Benzion. *The Origins of the Inquisition in Fifteenth Century Spain.* New York: Random House, 1995.

Neumann, Werner, and Hans-Joachim Schulze, eds. *Bach-Dokumente I: Schriftstücke von der Hand Johann Sebastian Bachs.* Cassel: Bärenreiter, 1963.

――――. *Bach-Dokumente II: Fremdschriftliche und gedruckte Dokumente zum Lebensgeschichte Johann Sebastian Bachs 1685–1750.* Cassel: Bärenreiter, 1969.

Neusner, Jacob. *The Mishnah before 70.* Atlanta: Scholars Press, 1987.

――――. *The Mishnah: Introduction and Reader.* Philadelphia: Trinity Press International, 1992.

――――. *A Rabbi Talks with Jesus: An Intermillennial, Interfaith Exchange.* New York: Doubleday, 1993.

―――― et al., eds. *Judaisms and Their Messiahs at the Turn of the Christian Era.* Cambridge: Cambridge University Press, 1987.

Oberman, Heiko A. *Luther: Man between God and the Devil,* trans. Eileen Wallise-Schwarzbart. New Haven: Yale University Press, 1989; German orig. 1982.

――――. *The Roots of Anti-Semitism in the Age of Renaissance and Reformation,* trans. James I. Porter. Philadelphia: Fortress, 1984; German orig. 1981.

Olearius, Johann. *Biblische Erklärung: Darinnen, nechst dem allgemeinen Haupt-Schlüssel der gantzen heiligen Schrifft.* Leipzig, 1678–81.
I consulted the exemplar owned by the Lutheran Theological Seminary in Philadelphia. Bach had a copy in his personal library. This reference Bible is especially useful, as it frequently also provides page references to commentaries in other books, including standard editions of Luther's works, several of which Bach owned. The manuscript list of books in Bach's library, which is a copy of a lost original (Leaver, *Bachs Theologische Bibliothek,* 30–35), reports that he owned Olearius in three volumes. He presumably had the entire five-part work bound in three massive volumes of well over 2,000 pages each (e.g., the way parts I–II are bound together in the copy in the library of the Lutheran Theological Seminary in Philadelphia [Leaver, *Bachs Theologische Bibliothek,* 82] and in various other copies [personal communication from Renate Steiger]). Some scholars suggest that Bach's three volumes most likely encompassed only the three parts containing the Hebrew Scriptures (e.g., Wallmann, "Johann Sebastian Bach und die 'Geistlichen Bücher' seiner Bibliothek," 170). They fail to

mention, however, that Olearius printed the Hebrew Scriptures in four parts and the New Testament in one. It seems rather unlikely, in any event, that Bach would have been unable to get a hold of the New Testament portion, as he had many acquaintances in theological circles, including Olearius families in Arnstadt and Leipzig (Neumann, *Bach-Dokumente II*, 21, 381). Also, Bach was intimately familiar with other materials by Olearius that are not listed in his library (Steiger, "J. S. Bachs Gebetbuch?").

Pagels, Elaine. *The Origin of Satan.* New York: Random House, 1995.

Pelikan, Jaroslav. *Bach among the Theologians.* Philadelphia: Fortress, 1986.

Petzoldt, Martin. *"Texte zur Leipziger Kirchen-Musik": Zum Verständnis der Kantatentexte Johann Sebastian Bachs.* Wiesbaden: Breitkopf and Härtel, 1993.

Pirro, André. *J. S. Bach,* trans. Mervyn Savill. New York: Orion, 1957; French orig. 1906; German ed. 1911.

Rupp, Gordon. *Martin Luther: Hitler's Cause — or Cure? In Reply to Peter F. Wiener.* London: Lutterworth, 1945.
A reply to Wiener, *Martin Luther: Hitler's Spiritual Ancestor.*

Saldarini, Anthony J. *Pharisees, Scribes and Sadducees in Palestinian Society: A Sociological Approach.* Wilmington: Glazier, 1988.

Sanders, E. P. *Jesus and Judaism.* Philadelphia: Fortress, 1985.

Schleuning, Peter. "'. . . auf daß zur heil'gen Liebe werde unser Haß' — Auf der Suche nach dem schwarzen Diamanten: Haß in der Musik." In *Haß: Die Macht eines unerwünschten Gefühls,* ed. Renate Kahle et al., 134–57. Reinbek: Rowohlt, 1985.

Schmieder, Wolfgang, ed. *Thematisch-systematisches Verzeichnis der musikalischen Werke von Johann Sebastian Bach: Bach-Werke-Verzeichnis (BWV).* Leipzig: Breitkopf and Härtel, 1950; rev. ed. Wiesbaden, 1990.

Schreckenberg, Heinz. *The Jews in Christian Art: An Illustrated History,* trans. John Bowden. New York: Continuum, 1996; German orig. 1996.

Schulenberg, David. "'Musical Allegory' Reconsidered: Representation and Imagination in the Baroque." *Journal of Musicology* 12 (1995): 203–39.

Schulze, Hans-Joachim. *Studien zur Bach–Überlieferung im 18. Jahrhundert.* Leipzig: Edition Peters, 1984.

Schulze, Hans-Joachim, and Christoph Wolff. *Bach Compendium,* vol. 1, pt. 3. Leipzig: Peters, 1988.

Schulze, Hans-Joachim, and Werner Neumann, eds. *Bach-Dokumente I: Schriftstücke von der Hand Johann Sebastian Bachs.* Cassel: Bärenreiter, 1963.

———, eds. *Bach-Dokumente II: Fremdschriftliche und gedruckte Dokumente zum Lebensgeschichte Johann Sebastian Bachs 1685–1750.* Cassel: Bärenreiter, 1969.

Sherman, Franklin, and Leon Klenicki. "Luther and Lutheranism on the Jews and Judaism: A Dialogue between Rabbi Leon Klenicki and Dr. Franklin Sherman." *Interfaith Focus* 2, no. 1 (1995): 1–18.
This publication is available from the Anti-Defamation League of B'nai B'rith, Department of Interfaith Affairs, 823 United Nations Plaza, New York, N.Y. 10017.

Shirer, William. *The Rise and Fall of the Third Reich.* New York: Simon and Schuster, 1960.

Sloyan, Gerard S. *The Crucifixion of Jesus: History, Myth, Faith.* Minneapolis: Fortress, 1995.

Smend, Friedrich. *Bach in Köthen,* trans. John Page, ed. Stephen Daw. St. Louis: Concordia, 1985; German orig. 1951.

———. "Bach und Luther" (orig. 1947). In Smend, *Bach-Studien: Gesammelte Reden und Aufsätze,* ed. Christoph Wolff, 153–75. Cassel: Bärenreiter, 1969.

Spitta, Philipp. *Johann Sebastian Bach,* vol. 2. Leipzig, 1880.

Stapert, Calvin. "Christus Victor: Bach's *St. John Passion.*" *Reformed Journal* 39, no. 3 (1989): 17–23.

Steiger, Lothar. "'Wir haben keinen König denn den Kaiser!' — Pilatus und die Juden in der Passionsgeschichte nach dem Johannesevangelium mit Bezug auf Heinrich Schütz und Johann Sebastian Bach: Oder die Frage nach dem Antijudaismus." *Musik und Kirche* 64 (1994): 264–71.

Steiger, Renate. "Bach und Israel." *Musik und Kirche* 50 (1980): 15–22.

———. "J. S. Bachs Gebetbuch? Ein Fund am Rande einer Ausstellung." *Musik und Kirche* 55 (1985): 231–34.

———. "'Wo soll ich fliehen hin?' Das Lied und Bachs Kantate BWV 5 — Theologische und musikalische Akzente in J. S. Bachs Passionen." In *"Wie freudig ist mein Herz, da Gott versöhnet ist" — Die Lehre von der Versöhnung in Kantaten und Orgelchorälen von Johann Sebastian Bach,* ed. Renate Steiger, 37–104. Heidelberg, 1995.

Sterne, Laurence. *The Life and Opinions of Tristram Shandy, Gentleman.* London, 1760–67.

Stiller, Günther. *Johann Sebastian Bach and Liturgical Life in Leipzig,* trans. Herbert J. A. Bouman et al., ed. Robin A. Leaver. St. Louis: Concordia, 1984; German orig. 1970.

Taruskin, Richard. "Facing Up, Finally, to Bach's Dark Vision" (orig. 1991). In Taruskin, *Text and Act: Essays on Music and Performance,* 307–15. New York: Oxford University Press, 1995.

———. "Text and Act" (orig. 1994). In Taruskin, *Text and Act: Essays on Music and Performance,* 353–58. New York: Oxford University Press, 1995.

Telemann, Georg Philipp. *St. John Passion: "Music vom Leiden und Sterben des Welterlösers,"* libretto by Joachim Zimmerman. Nuremberg, 1745–49.

Terry, Charles Sanford. *Bach: The Passions,* vol. 1. Westport: Greenwood, 1971; orig. 1926.

———. *Joh. Seb. Bach: Cantata Texts, Sacred and Secular; with a Reconstruction of the Leipzig Liturgy of his Period.* London: Holland Press, 1964; orig. 1926.

Tomita, Yo. *http://www.music.qub.ac.uk/~tomita/bachbib.html*
An on-line bibliography of writings on Bach; established but not yet available as of this writing.

Trachtenberg, Joshua. *The Devil and the Jews: The Medieval Conception of the Jew and its Relation to Modern Antisemitism.* New Haven: Yale University Press, 1943.

Urban, Linwood. *A Short History of Christian Thought: Revised & Expanded Edition.* New York: Oxford University Press, 1995.

Van der Horst, Pieter W. "The Birkat ha-minim in Recent Research." *Expository Times* 105 (1994): 363–68.

Vollständiges Kirchen-Buch. Leipzig, 1731.

Von Loewenich, Walther. *Luther's Theology of the Cross,* trans. Herbert J. A. Bouman. Minneapolis: Augsburg, 1976.

Wallmann, Johannes. "Johann Sebastian Bach und die 'Geistlichen Bücher' seiner Bibliothek." *Pietismus und Neuzeit* 12 (1986): 162–81.

———. "The Reception of Luther's Writings on the Jews from the Reformation to the End of the 19th Century." *Lutheran Quarterly* (new series) 1, no. 1 (1987): 72–97. Reprinted in *Stepping-Stones to Further Jewish-Lutheran Relationships: Key Lutheran Statements,* ed. Harold H. Ditmanson. Minneapolis: Augsburg, 1990.

Walter, Meinrad. "Die Bibel, Bach, die Juden — und wir: Zum Verständnis der Johannes-Passion Bachs (BWV 245)." *Württembergische Blätter für Kirchenmusik* 60 (1993): 210–12.

Weise, Christian. *Der grünen Jugend Nothwendige Gedancken.* Leipzig, 1675.

Westerholm, Stephen. *Israel's Law and the Church's Faith: Paul and his Recent Interpreters.* Grand Rapids: Eerdmans, 1988.

Wiener, Peter F. *Martin Luther: Hitler's Spiritual Ancestor.* London: Hutchinson, 1945.

Wolff, Christoph, ed. *Bach-Bibliographie: Nachdruck der Verzeichnisse des Schrifttums über Johann Sebastian Bach (Bach-Jahrbuch 1905–1984); mit einem Supplement und Register.* Cassel: Merseburger, 1985.

Wolff, Christoph, and Hans-Joachim Schulze. *Bach Compendium,* vol. 1, pt. 3. Leipzig: Peters, 1988.

Index of Movements from Bach's *St. John Passion*

Index of Bach's Works

Index of Biblical and Other Ancient Sources

Index of Names and Subjects